Lost and Turned Out

Lost and Turned Out

Toni Shealey

To order additional copies of this book, contact:
Xlibris Corporation
1-888-795-4274
www.Xlibris.com
Orders@Xlibris.com
83703

CONTENTS

Acknowledgements

WOW! THIS IS absolutely unbelievable. Never in a million years did I think that I would be here. All I've ever wanted to do was write, and express what I felt. First, and foremost I have to thank God because without him none of this would have been possible. To my friends and family that supported me through this all thank you for your support and encouragement along the way.

I would like to thank all of the talented people that help me put all these pieces together for "Lost and Turned Out". My partner, Joette Keller. My sisters, Patrice Smith, Bonita Threatt Bothwell, Elinita Scott and my brother, Glennon Threatt. Gone but never forgotten my mother Patricia McCracken, and my grandmother Mary A. Arnold who are no longer with us in body, but will always be with us in spirit. Without you two I wouldn't have had my story.

To my children, Willie, Patricia, Anthony, Hassan, Lee and Cadesia. Who inspired me from the day that they were born. My nephews, Greg, Taevon, and my niece Diona who believed in me. And my great niece Madison who gave us all life. I love you all so much. Also, to all of my friends who read and reread my manuscript, pushing me forward when I thought I just couldn't do it anymore. They believed in me when I didn't believe in myself. To Xlibris Publications for your excellent work. Thank you.

Part 1

Victim

1969-1981

"S HEALEY, YOU'VE GOT mail!" the correctional officer calls as I get out of the shower. I was being held in Medina County Jail, a holding facility in Medina Ohio for federal inmates. My charge was bank fraud and identity theft.

As I'm drying off a tune by Natalie Cole, plays in my head. "Growing up, it wasn't easy for Annie Mae." "A little girl, in a great big world. Annie Mae. "She was growing up much too fast." "Somebody's got to stop her!" "Oh, Annie, Annie, Annie Mae . . ." The song makes me sad and melancholy; it's as if I was reliving my childhood all over again. The memories engulf me. Just like it was only yesterday.

I kept trying to figure out how it all came to this. As the song continues to play in my head, I was amazed at how much Annie Mae and my life was the same. The day I was born I already had two strikes against me, I was a female and I was black. I was born June 2, 1966, Tonineti Arnold to Patricia Ann Arnold.

We lived in a housing project in Birmingham Alabama called Collegeville. My mom had six brothers and three sisters and we all stayed with my grandma who I called mama, and everyone in the neighborhood called Ms. Mary. I loved my uncles so much because they spoiled me rotten and they really took care of me.

My mother was a mystery to me. Sometimes I would see her and sometimes I didn't. It didn't bother me at the time, I had so much love around me I thought that this was how life was suppose to be, and because I was so young I had no idea what was going on around me.

The majority of the time I was at my grandma's house. There was always something going on in our house. My grandma worked at Carver High School in the lunchroom. Mama was a great cook, and was known for the cinnamon rolls she made. Up until this day in order for me to make someone that went to Carver remember who my grandma was, I have to say the lady that made the cinnamon rolls. Students actually called her the cinnamon roll lady.

On Friday's grandma sold liquor out of her house, back then it was called a bootleg house. Around five in the evening you could hear the men coming in our back door from work at the steel plant. There would be so many things going on at one time. My uncles would all have their friends over. They'd all be in the back room. You could hear the men my grandma was serving, yell loudly "Mary let me get a fifty cent shot." If I was lucky as they were pulling out their money I'd get handed a quarter. You could smell the fish and chicken wings my grandma was cooking a mile away. My friends and I would be out back playing "Mother May I", "Simon Said" and "Hide and seek". We had numerous games that we shared, and at three and four years old I didn't have a care in the world.

My grandma was also the candy lady of the neighborhood. She sold freeze cups for a dime, or you could get an ice-cream cone, now and laters, you name it she sold it. My friend's and I favorite thing to do were to turn our freeze cups upside down and suck the Kool-Aid juice out the top of the ice.

I was a very friendly little girl, and I was always getting compliments about how pretty I was or how pretty my hair was. I was very mischievous too and I got my share of whippings.

In 1971, my mother was pregnant with my sister, Trice. I remember feeling a little upset because I thought that all the attention would be on the new baby and no one would love me anymore. Actually, it was the complete opposite. From the day my sister was born I claimed her as mine. She was a fat little bald headed baby and I thought that she was the most beautiful thing in the world.

Both of our father's identities would be questionable throughout our life. My mother had several relationships, and whenever I asked her who my father was she always stated "Whoever paid the most."

Today I know why my grandma was insistent about keeping me with her. My mom was on drugs and involved in a bunch of other things which I wouldn't find out about until I was an adult. Eventually, she disappeared again and left my sister with my grandma. We found out that she was living with her lover a lady named Pat. At that time I didn't know what "bull dyke" was but my grandma said it so much until I finally realized that my mother was in a relationship with another woman, and according to my grandma it was the worst thing in the world. Pat was really nice to me, and I'd spend mostly weekends at their apartment. They stayed across the street from Legion Field which is where a lot of football games and other entertainment are held in Birmingham.

I loved my little life; the years that I had been in this world had been good to me. I had graduated from daycare, started going to elementary school and was eager to learn.

In 1973 my life would change and there was no turning back. It had been written, that this was a journey I would take in my life and it would shape me into the woman I am today.

We moved out of the project to a suburban neighborhood called Norwood. As the black families were moving in the white ones were moving out. There was so much going on in the world, racism, segregation. Martin Luther King, the 16th street Baptist Church bombing. I didn't have a clue that history was being made around me. After we got settled in my sister, uncles, grandma and I, it became home again. I was enrolled in Norwood Elementary School, second grade. I loved school. School was where I flourished and absorbed knowledge. I was very athletic I was involved in all kinds of sports. Three years in a row. I won best athletic girl for participating in all of the school sports events. I wanted to try out for volleyball, track, and basketball but grandma always had an excuse about why I couldn't.

The year I turned eight was when I lost my childhood and was forced to view this world as a woman in a child body. Every day I came home from school my uncles would be sitting on the front porch. I could always count on them giving me money, because they would want me to run to the store for them, or not to tell my grandma that they had their girl friends in the house.

This one particular day I came home, it was as if a dark cloud was hanging over our house. My uncles weren't on the porch; I didn't hear the radio or the laughter. I walked into the house and there was a strange man sitting at our kitchen table. My grandma introduced him to me as her husband. Over the next two or three weeks, I would find out that he was my grandma's first husband, also the father of her three oldest children, who throughout my life I had only seen periodically. I found out also that they had been separated for thirty years, and that my mom, her sister, and other five brothers were by my biological grandfather, who everyone called Capp.

As W.C. became a permanent fixture in our house things slowly began to change. There was no more laughter; my grandma was constantly telling us to hold it down. She even put a lock on the deep freezer because she didn't want us to eat "His food." W.C. worked at Loveman's Warehouse. He left for work early every morning, and he got home around eight p.m. He never said much to any of us, and if he did say something he said it through my grandma.

Eventually, my uncles started leaving, because they were young men and didn't feel like he could tell them what to do. After a while there was only me, and my sister. Three of my mother's younger brothers stayed but they came and went as they pleased. Pee was my mama's favorite brother; sadly he was the one I had to be weary of. We had one big room in our house, and in that room were two beds. My sister and I would sleep in that bed with my uncle in the other. Some nights he would crawl into bed with me and grind up against my behind, then take his hand and rub my vagina. I was so scared; because I knew in my mind that what he was doing wasn't suppose to be happening. I always got really cold and nervous whenever I was left alone with him but I didn't know what to say or who to say it to. I have always wondered as I grew into adulthood was it something that I did to attract this kind of attention. But then I wondered who would be attracted to a seven year child anyway?

That was the beginning of my self-esteem going down. At that point I didn't want to be the center of attention anymore, and I did everything that I could to stay out of every ones way.

I remember one night my mom had just come into town. She would do that all the time show up in the middle of the night with her husband James, and they would bring us toys, money, all kinds of nice things. I would be so excited. Half of the time I couldn't contain myself. I thought my mama was the prettiest lady in the whole world. Her hair was long wavy, she had the prettiest smile, and she always smelled good.

Now on this particular night I had made my mind up. I was going to tell my mom about Pee. I called out to my mom, "Mama, Pee was feeling on me." But everyone was talking so loud; I don't think she heard exactly what I said because as a second thought she turned to me and asked, "What did you say? I looked over to my uncle and he looked at me with the most evil look I had seen. You have to understand I was only eight years old, and he scared the shit out of me. The next morning it was brought to my attention that my mama was feeling maternal. So she was going to take me, my sister and Pee out of town with them for the summer. Pee and my sister were ecstatic, and in a way I was too. I thought that this trip would give me an opportunity to spend some time with my mom, or so I thought.

I remember it took us a while to get to our destination but I was so excited because I was able to see the surroundings as we drove up the highway. After all the driving we finally made it to Charlotte, North Carolina and we lived in a very pretty apartment complex. There was a swimming pool, tennis courts, and beautiful green grass and trees. Our apartment had two bedrooms. My sister and I had our own room, my uncle slept downstairs. Me and my sister was so overwhelmed with being and living with our mom that we were about to burst. It was only a matter of time before things started to change. I would hear my mama and James arguing about money. Then mama would wake up sometimes really angry then we would see her later on and she would be nice again. As time progressed, I would learn that mama was angry because she hadn't got her heroin and nice when she did. Little things that my sister and I did would just irk her and she would scream and curse at us. I remember my sister is left handed and that's the hand she used to eat with. At dinner time my mom would beat my sister's left hand until she picked up the right and start using it. There was another time, I didn't have any clean clothes to put on, but ironically I wore the same size as my mom. She told me to get something out of her closet to wear and I did a blouse and a jean skirt. I guess she forgot because she came in the room screaming and cursing "Who told you to put on my mother fucking clothes?" I was so nervous that I made a mistake and didn't answer quickly enough, and she slapped me and told me to "Take her shit off." This kind of behavior went on for quite awhile. One day mama and James told us that they were going out of town and they would return in about a week. Well, they left Pee in charge of my Trice and I, and I almost shitted on me because I would be alone in this house with my uncle. Anyway, they left that day and they left enough food that would last us for about a week. That first week they were gone, I don't think I slept a wink, because I thought Pee would try to touch me again. When I realize that he wasn't. I was able to let my guard down and have fun. My sister and I went swimming everyday and would run around with the kids we had met there. At the end of our first week alone, I noticed that we were running out of food, it was okay though because my mama said that they should be back around this time. After the first week Pee took the twenty-five they left for him and bought us food but that soon ran out. I would run over to the seven-eleven and steal bologna and hotdogs. So we would have some food. Then when that ran out, I would get a screw driver and open other tenant's doors and steal food out of their refrigerators. One time I stole some meat off someone's grill. After about a week and a half my mama finally showed up, and we packed up and left in the middle of the night without paying the rent.

The next stop was Atlanta, Georgia. We were living in some apartments with friends of my mama and James. Things rapidly went down hill from there. My mother would take me and Trice to the mall, go in a store, fill up the bag and make us walk out with them. I would cry so badly, because somehow I knew this was wrong. My mama and James would fight everyday and when they weren't fighting they were shooting dope and nodding. If my Trice or I got in the way we would get slapped or knocked down. I finally got a chance to slip off and call my grandma and let her know what was going on. She then informed my mama that if she didn't send us back on the next thing smoking that she'd call the police. Pee and Trice were really sad. I felt like if I never see them again, I wouldn't be mad at all. From that point on anytime my mama came to town, I wouldn't go anywhere with her.

Summer was almost over we would be going back to school after Labor Day. I was ready to go back too! Once we started school everything went back to the way it was. Now it was only me my sister, my grandma, and W.C. Pee left to go live with my mama, where ever that was.

Once everything was back in the swing Trice and I were back in school, grandma and W.C worked all during the week also. On Friday my grandma would send me across the street to Ms. Minnie house. Ms Minnie was the neighborhood bootleg house. Grandma always sent for the same thing six tall Miller beers. It would take me at least thirty minutes to get to Ms. Minnie's door because she had lots of cats and I was deathly afraid of cats. Grandma would take her beer in the back room with her and for the next two days she would dance, laugh and have her self a ball. Some Fridays she went to club meetings, or over her sister-in-law's house. Club meetings was where grandma and all of her friends got together and talked about upcoming events they were putting together and would be attending.

On these nights W.C would stop at the liquor store on his way home. Once he got home he'd drink, talk shit, and be more sociable than he would during the week. On Fridays I could hear him in their room talking to him and cursing. Sometimes he would go out back and shoot his gun up in the air. I had over heard my grandma talking over the phone telling someone that he had been "shell shocked" while he was in the army. I can remember my Aunt, mom's baby sister complaining about him. Telling grandma that she should do something about him, and grandma would always say the same thing "Y'all know that man is crazy!" That was her excuse for his behavior. Then one Friday, I'll never forget it, because that's when my world was turned upside down. Trice was at her godmother's house in Collegeville, and my grandma was at club meeting. There was no one in the house but me and W.C. Around this time of evening is when my mother's two youngest brothers would drop by and be in and out. I was in my room sitting on my bed watching Sanford and Son. It was a show that came on every Friday night. I loved watching it because Redd Foxx was very funny to me.

I could see W.C. out of the corner of my eyes. He was walking in the hallway, with nothing but his boxer shorts on coming towards the door. I tried hard not to look at him, tried not to blink, but when I opened my eyes he was standing directly in front of me. Before I knew what was going on he had grabbed me and put his hand over my mouth, I smelled the liquor on his breath as he talked. I thought "is this a game?" In the next instance, I knew it wasn't. He pushed me onto the bed and straddled me mumbling, unintelliable words. I was so afraid and did not understand what was going on. He ripped my shorts and my panties. I felt something wet and hard on my leg, then he entered me and it felt as if someone had ripped my insides out. Tears were running down my face. I was hoping and praying that someone would come in and help me. Then I tried to figured out if I had done some wrong that day, and this was some kind of punishment, the last thing I remembered was hearing the music from Sanford and Son as it went off, and him telling me before I blacked out, "If you tell, I'll kill your sister!" How could he know that my sister was all I had to call my own, and that I would do anything to protect her? When I woke up. I was hoping I had had a bad dream, but when I moved my legs the excruciating pain let me know that it wasn't a dream it was definitely real. I went in the bathroom and cleaned myself up, put my tore up underwear, shorts, and the blanket in a garbage bag and took it out to the alley. As I walked past his room I could hear him in there snoring. I went on got in my bed and cried myself to sleep.

The abuse went on continuously. Never the same, he would make me perform oral sex on him or have anal sex whichever one suited him at the time. Most of the time my sister would be home, so I'd put her in another room so he wouldn't bother her. That was my way to trying to protect her. By 1975, I had become very withdrawn. I had started to think something was really wrong with me or why else would this man keep doing this to me? I felt like everyone was staring at me. My mama was away in prison. Sometimes she'd call home and I'd asked her over and over when are you coming home? I always got the same answer, soon. I had developed a really bad attitude and nothing that anyone said could put out this anger in me. I did not know where it was coming from; all I know is that it was there.

I was so tired, I could not sleep, and the memories just kept running through my head, trying to figure out what went wrong, or even what I could have done to prevent it. As my roommate lie over in her bed and sleep, I envy her the peace because I can't shake these demons.

I remember thinking, if there is a God why is this happening to me? I was angry all the time. I started skipping school. So on top of W.C. constant sexual abuse, my grandma made him the disciplinarian. This one particular Sunday night we had a recreation center that all the kids went to after church. My grandma had told me if you go to church you can't go to the center and vise versa. I took upon myself and stayed to both. When I got home my grandma and W.C. were standing on the front porch waiting for me. He told me to take my coat off because he was going to whip me. I ran out the door, up out of my shoes. I ran until I couldn't run no more. Finally when I thought there was no one chasing me I began to walk. I did not know where I was going all I know is that I had to get away from them.

In the beginning I had no idea where I was going then it came to me. I'll go to my Aunt house. So I walked from Norwood to Collegeville with nothing but my coat, dress and stockings on. I had peed on myself and it was really cold. From our house to my Aunts was a long ass walk. I was so scared but not scared enough to be afraid of someone taking me off and doing something to me. When I got to my aunts house she opened the door. I was crying so hard she could hardly understand what I was saying. I finally calmed down enough to tell her that W.C. had whipped me. My auntie looked at me like are you sure that's all that happened? I immediately remembered the threat, I said yes. She took me back home. My grandma gave her, her rendition of what happened and that was the end of that.

In the next couple of months I would continue to run away. I remember trying to poison them praying for them to die. I poured some green alcohol and turpentine in the soup my grandma was cooking knowing they would truly die then. I just wouldn't let my sister eat none. I didn't know that all those two liquids would do was stink up the house. When that didn't work I tried to set the house on fire. I was so hurt and angry. On top of that I couldn't tell anyone what was going on which was even worse because the anger was festering inside of me. My auntie noticed that something was wrong with me, so she brought it to my grandma's attention. Auntie approached grandma one day and said "mama something's wrong with Toni." My grandma said "ain't nothing wrong with her grown ass. She's going to be nothing, just like her mammy" which she never failed to tell me on a daily basis.

Finally, after I had run away a couple more times the warden of the prison let my mama come home on pass in August, 1976. I had just turned ten two months before. My mama was out on an eight hour pass from prison to see if she could talk some sense into me. We went to Wendy's, she asked me over and over again why I was behaving the way I was. I didn't say anything. Then she told me "If you don't go home Toni, they're going to put you in juvenile" I told her "I'd rather go to juvenile than to go back in that house." It would be years later that I found out he had also molested my little sister after I left. By the time I found out he was already dead because surely had he been alive, I would have killed him.

I was put in juvenile in a unit they called the Shelter Cottage for runaways. It would be there that I learned about personal hygiene, my cycle, and smoked my first cigarette. The prison had started letting my mom take her eight hour passes on Tuesday because that was my court dates. When I knew she was coming I'd break out of the Shelter Cottage run away, and then go back to juvenile when I knew she had went back to prison. On one of the nights that I ran away, a girl I met while in juvenile, from Tuscaloosa ran with me. I went over my god sister's house and we stayed there for a couple of days.

One night my friend and I were out and we ended up meeting these two guys. She told me that she knew them. We got in the car with them and we drove to a secluded spot not to far from Central City, a housing project in Birmingham. She was in the front seat with one guy, and I was in the back with the other. They were up front kissing and fondling each other. I felt really uncomfortable because I knew that this guy would want me to do the same. After a while he tried to pull me over to him, I got angry and jumped out of the car. Well when I turned around the guy from the front seat was running behind me saying "Come on we're going to take you home." Once

I got back in the back seat of the car, he got back there with me. He slapped me pretty hard and said "Bitch you're gonna give me some pussy." I fought with everything I had. After a while I just laid there and let him finish raping me! I remember feeling very lonely already, this just added on to my spiraling self-esteem, the feeling that I would rather die than to be in this world . . . "She was growing up much too fast. Annie Mae . . .

By the time that I was eleven years old, I had been in and out of every group home in Birmingham. By now they had me seeing a psychiatrist because not only was I bad, I was crazy also. We would have this therapy group, the doctor, me, my mother, my aunt, and my grandma. They all would sit there and ask me questions. I would tuned them out! Even as my mom sat there and cried and begged. My only thoughts were "I wish they would leave me the fuck alone." When I needed them to be there for me and they weren't. I was tired and my little heart was defeated. Can you imagine being eleven years old and feeling like you had the whole world on your shoulder.

I had made up my mind that I was going to tell the judge what had happened to me. Because I was tired and I wanted this burden off of me. Finally, my court date came around. My mom was up on another pass, my grandma and my auntie all came to court this day. When the judge asked me what was wrong. I blurted it out really fast, "W.C. was having sex with me." My grandma jumped up and said, "She's telling a goddamn lie!" She could have shot me in my chest, it wouldn't have hurt more than that statement she made. Nobody questioned me, or looked into what I had said. From that point on something inside of me completely shut down. I vowed to myself that nothing and nobody would ever hurt me again, no matter what. It was me against the world! Fuck'em, fuck all of them.

In 1977, I had started hanging out with some kids from the north side who stole cars. We would steal cars off of car lots. Sometimes we would joy ride but most of the time we sold them to this guy in North Birmingham. Of course he would cheat us, but shit we were young and once he paid us, we felt like we were on top of the world. A lot of times we would be in high speed chases, once the police caught us they would take us to juvenile and we would get right out. By this time I had started having sex which wasn't such a big deal to me being that I had already been molested and raped.

My mom had been released from prison and was staying with her lover Lula. One evening, a friend of mine name Red and I decided that we were

going to ride over to Atlanta with a couple of guys we had met in j[...]
They talked about getting money and stealing cars and we decided tha[...]
would ride with them to Atlanta and make some money. The whole tim[...]
we were riding in the car, one of the older guys Clee, kept staring at me
through the rearveiw mirror. Once we got to Atlanta he went in to rent a
room for us because we were all under age, and he was twenty. When we
got the room we forgot that nobody had cigarettes so everyone left out of
the room except Clee and me. Clee walked over to the dresser where I was
sitting and started running his fingers through my hair. I moved away from
him. The next thing I know he had punched me in the face and I started
screaming at me to take my clothes off. He hit me in my stomach I fell on
to the floor. Then he reached down and dragged me by my hair onto the
bed. He pulled out a switch blade and put it to my neck, he said "Bitch pull
off your pants" in my ear so I shut down. While he was raping me I just laid
there and went to that place in my mind where no one could hurt me. The
other three guys came in and took a turn after him. My friend came to the
door, and she asked "What are ya'll doing? That girl isn't but twelve years
old!" I vaguely remember Clee saying "I thought she was seventeen." I
thought to myself, "Would it have fucking mattered? The guys kept trying
to get me to get back in the car. I said "I'd rather walk to Birmingham
than to get back in the car with them." They left but Red stayed with me.
We didn't have a clue as to how we would get back to Birmingham. So we
walked the streets of Atlanta, until we met this couple. They were in town
for a convention and they were staying at the Peachtree Hotel. They seen
the condition I was in, invited us back to their room. They both were really
nice. Red explained to them what had happened to me. The lady ran me
a bath and asked if we had any relatives that they could call. I gave them
my mom telephone number. I don't know what was said. But after I had
bathed and put on fresh clothes. The people took us to the Greyhound bus
station and put both of us on a bus back to Birmingham.

When I got home my mama was in the bathroom, she came out went
into her room and came out with an extension cord. Not one time did she
ask me what happened or asked me how I was doing? I would have given
anything for my mama to hug me and tell me she loved me, anything!
She swung at me twice with the extension cord and missed, then she just
dropped it on the floor and she started crying. I just turned around and
went back out the door. Little did we know we wouldn't see each other for
a year. The guy that I was seeing at the time had gotten out of jail, and in
order for me to stay with him I had to sleep in the car at night in front of

ter his mama went to work we would go in the house to
sex. The last time we would steal cars together came
78. We had cased this lot out in Shelby County that
ss custom made vans. The dealer always left the keys
f us got in a van. As soon as we crunk up the vans the
lights on the car lot came on. Police were everywhere. You would
think we had enough sense to get out of the vans and surrender. We didn't!
Everybody pulled off the lot. It was something like Starsky and Hutch
high speed chase. We were going in every direction flying up highway 280.
All of us got caught that night. Because me, and Red was minors we were
held to be sent to Columbiana County Jail. It was a new facility. We were
housed in the part of the jail for juveniles. The guys were tried as adults.

I ended up going to a co-ed group home in Chalkville, Alabama. Once
I got there. I was very belligerent, I didn't trust anybody. Basically I was
just hurting and didn't know how to explain exactly what I was feeling. So
when I got mad, I'd throw shit, or turn the fish tank over. There was one
counselor there that took me under her wing, and no matter what I did
she would always tell me that whatever it was that I was going through that
she would always be there for me. There were other counselors there as
well that really gave a fuck about us. But a lot of the children there were so
messed up with family issues, that we really didn't trust anybody. I felt that
if I had let anyone get close to me all they would do is hurt me or leave me.

If I could do my life all over again, I would change the fact that I didn't
trust them. I don't regret any part of my life but that. Because today I know
if I had trusted them, those chosen few women would have helped me.

I stayed at Chalkville six months. Every time I got a chance to go home
on a pass I ran away again. Until they finally said, fuck it. I was thirteen
now and you couldn't tell me shit. I was grown. Around this time I started
hanging down on Sixteenth Street in Fountain Heights. That's where I
met my first love Junior. That boy could look at me and make me act like
a damn fool. Later, I would remember he was one of the boys that raped
me, but by then it would be too late. Junior was a jewelry, and fur thief.
He kept money he stayed sharp and he kept me sharp. His sister, Carmelita
and I became really close friends. Actually everyone thought Carmelita and
I were sisters. His mother Ms. Bee always told me if Junior and I ever broke
up I would always be her daughter. Junior and I over the next couple of
months became inseparable.

Then he started to change. He started accusing me of cheating on him,
at first it would be a push. Then it got out of hand. If a phone call came

in and it was the wrong number, he'd swear to God that it was some one calling for me. If we were walking somewhere and a guy looked at me I had to be "fucking" him. During the time that these incidents would happen, he would beat me, make me take my clothes off and beat me with clothes hangers. A lot of times I was able to run away and hide at my grandma's house because I had nowhere else to go.

One particular night I went home. I was tired of him beating on me. I lay down in the den of my grandma's house. When I woke up the next morning he was standing over my head beating me in the head with his shoe. I found out later that he got in the turned house because my great grandfather had Alzheimer's and he thought that Junior was one of my uncles. Junior then stole jewelry and two of my grandma's televisions so that she could think I stole them, and stop me from coming to her house. Well, it worked my grandma issued a warrant for me for burglary, and the next two years I wouldn't be able to go home. I ended up staying with him. Junior got tired of Birmingham and said we needed a change. We ended up going to Fayetteville, North Carolina. His cousin was stationed there and we lived with him. One morning I woke up and Junior and his cousin were in the front room talking. After I brushed my teeth and washed my face I went into the living room. Junior turned to be and said "five guys from the Army Base are coming over tonight and you're going to turn a trick with them." I said "No the fuck I ain't!" He said, "Bitch your gonna do exactly what the fuck I said. Or I'll break your motherfucking back. "I was so scared because the type of dude Junior was, if I didn't do what he said he was going to fuck me up. I tried to come up with a plan to leave, but my mind kept telling me that if I left he would eventually find me. Unfortunately he didn't leave the house all day. I guess he felt in his heart if he left that I would run.

Around six p.m. Junior came in the back room and gave me a red see through gown with two splits up the sides. This dude had really thought this shit out. He then gave me two Valiums and told me to take them after I got out of the shower, because they'd make me relax. Then this he had the audacity to hug me and say "You know I love you right?" You're doing this for us. If I had a gun I would have blown his motherfucking brains out. In the shower I cried and I cried it felt like my soul had been ripped out of my body. There was no way out. But the worst part was realizing that he really didn't give a fuck about me, and that hurt more than anything in this world, because of he was my world. As I got older I learned to realize that men only wanted me for the things that I could do for them and the sad part about it I didn't care I just wanted to belong.

When I finished showering, I went through the motions of putting on lotion I took the two Valiums, and as I did my hair, I made myself believe what Junior was saying. I was doing this for us.

As, I was coming out of the bathroom I could hear voices in the front room. Junior seen me come out, and followed me into the bedroom. He gave me a watch and told me "Don't let them motherfuckers go over fifteen minutes a piece!" As soon as he walked out a huge white dude came in looking all goofy and shit. I told him he had fifteen minutes to do what he had to do. I wasn't going to help him. When that man got on top of me, and I looked at the watch in my hand, I wanted to die. You can not imagine how low and degrading I felt. I just wanted to DIE! The next hour went by in a blur. I remember, I told one dude that his time was up. He told me he wasn't finished I told him "That's not my motherfucking problem so get out!" I found out later that his cousin had set up the transactions and that the dude's had to pay two hundred dollars a piece for fifteen minutes. After they left I went in the bathroom to wash that fucking filth off of me. I thought if I could scrub this shit off I'd be okay. I stayed in that shower until I was raw. Then I looked up into the cabinet and the first bottle of pills I saw I took them and I kept taking them.

When I woke up Junior was slapping me in the face and trying to get me to drink milk. After he got me to throw up a few times I fell back into a deep sleep. I might have slept two or three days. I don't know. All I know is that my head was hurting really bad and my mouth felt like cotton. Junior came in when he heard me stirring around. He said "you're a dumb, stupid ass bitch. You didn't have enough sense to kill yourself right. I just laid here and continued to cry. But I had made up my mind as soon as they both left out of the house. I'm gone. My opportunity came later on that evening. I called my grandma and asked her could she pay for me a bus ticket. She said I would have to wait until Friday because that's when she got paid. I hung up from her. I started panicking. I had to get out of this house before they got back I turned that house upside down looking for money. Finally I looked under the couch and I seen a shaving kit bag. I pulled it from under there, unzipped it. And lo and behold. There was money and bags of weed. I called the bus station to see how much the ticket was, and then I asked what time the next bus left. They told me three fourty eight p.m. and it was two thirty pm already. I took fifty dollars out of the bag, enough to get my ticket, pay the cab and get me something to eat. I called a cab and prayed that it would get there on time. All the time thinking that if Junior caught me he was going to kill me. The cab came, he got me to the bus station at three-thirty just enough time to catch the bus. Once the bus pulled out I exhaled a little, but still was petrified that he would catch me.

The whole ride back to Birmingham, I kept thinking that when I looked back I would see Juniors cousin little yellow Toyota following the bus.

As I look back on that time I remember feeling, scared, betrayed, and lost. It seemed like I was always carrying around a whole bunch of shit. At that time I didn't think there was anyone I could talk to so the feelings just stayed inside and festered. After I was home for about a week. I went to the clinic because I wasn't feeling good. When they finished doing the exam the nurse called me and my auntie to the back and told me I was pregnant. My aunt said, "Toni you have one or two options, you can have the baby or have an abortion, but whatever you do I'll stand by your side and help you as much as I can." My aunt was the only one in my life that I trusted whole heartedly. For some reason I wasn't mad at her like I was everyone else. It was like she knew something and tried her best to protect me from it, when she could. She eventually seen that I would continue to run the streets and she kept me with her as much as possible.

Her logic was if she took me out with her then at least she'd be able to watch me, as opposed to me being out in the clubs and stuff alone. I told her everything except what I had went through in my grandma's house. W.C. still had the fear of God in me because my sister still stayed in that house. He wouldn't approach me now because I was big enough to fend for myself.

As time progressed I realized that he only preyed on small girls, that couldn't defend themselves.

I decided to have the baby, but as faith would have it I miscarried, June eighth nineteen-eighty two. Six days after I turned fifteen. With me having the attitude I had, that didn't faze me. I went right on with my life as if nothing had happened. A couple of months later Junior came back to Birmingham of course I got back with him. I loved him, and he continued to beat me and it seemed now that it was worst than before. He had my dumb ass really believing that he truly loved me. That if I wouldn't do stuff to make him so mad, then he wouldn't beat me. It was sad because I actually thought all men beat their women. Hell, I had seen my step father beat my mama lots of times. Then they would get back together. We were living what you call the "hustler's life" and in the life the men always called their women bitches and hoes and the women also gave money to their men. When they came from work. The work consisted of hoeing, boosting, playing the con game, forgery, whatever. My mama, my stepfather and my three uncles played the con game. Everybody downtown knew my family. So for the men I was a good prospect because I cam from a hustling family.

In August of 1982, I went to juvenile for boosting. Me knowing these people were gong to send me back to girl school, I had to think of something fast. Junior had even come to try and break me out, but he almost got caught. I came up with the idea that the girls in my unit would call Ms. Roberts, a day counselor, in to get them some toilet paper out of the closet. Once she turned her back I was suppose to take my shoe laces and put them around Ms. Robert's neck. They called her in and soon as she went to open the door. I put the laces around her neck. I must have been choking her really hard, because she was turning red in the face and the girls started beating on the window hollering for the other counselor on duty, saying that I was trying to kill Ms. Roberts. About seven male counselors came because by this time I had let Ms. Roberts go and picked up a mop ringer, and started swinging at the girls. They finally got me cuffed. Next thing I know I was being transferred to the county jail. My charge was attempted murder, but Ms. Roberts wouldn't press charges because she said she knew me and that she had literally raised me, since I had been coming in and out of juvenile. I stayed in the county jail four days before I was released on bond. Junior and Ms. Bee had found a crooked lawyer that all the hustlers in Birmingham used. We would give him jewelry, furs, clothes. You name it, he took it. Years later he would be tried and convicted also for unrelated charges. There was also a judge, who worked with our attorney. Regardless of what our case was if we got in front of this judge our case was getting thrown out. But by July 1983, the judge had got tired of seeing me in his court room and he sentenced me to three years, in the state penitentiary for women.

Of the three years I would only serve one year.

A couple of months before I got sentenced Junior had already been sent to the penitentiary. After sentencing I stayed in the county jail two weeks before they transferred me to Julia Tutwiler Prison for women. Because I was only sixteen they housed me in the trustee block.

TONI SHEALEY

I met a lady named Liz who I called mom, because she looked after me and made sure that I was alright. She told me not take anything from anybody because if you do they'll make you their woman. Being the feisty individual that I was I said "Ain't nobody gone to fuck with me!" When we arrived at the prison we were taken into the infirmary because that was where you went when you first got to prison. All inmates had to spend at least two to three weeks until the nurses ran the entire physical test on you like pap smears, urine, dental, pulling blood. Once the test results came back negative you were then placed in population. By me being sixteen I was considered fresh meat for lesbians.

While walking down the hall to the infirmary inmates were lined up against the wall saying things like "PYT" pretty young thang "I'm gone have you", "You finer than a mother fucker." I just kept looking straight ahead cause I had made it up in my mind, that if one of them hoes pull up on me I was gonna bust them in their face. At sixteen I had real long hair, small breast, and my ass was thicker than a motherfucker. The whole three weeks I was in the infirmary. I got kites (letters) faithfully. Females would come back there telling other females that were in the infirmary with me "Tell that lil young girl to come to the door" I would get so angry cause I didn't go that way! Finally, the day came for me to go out into population. On the inside I was shaking like a leaf but on the outside, I wasn't afraid of shit.

My mom had been in this prison before so a lot of her friends (old timers) knew about me (Lil Pat's daughter) and other females that I had known from the streets were trying to holla at me too. In my mind I was like "damn I didn't know she went that way."

Once I got settled in to the prison routine the old timers put me up on the do's and don'ts. I enrolled in Trade School to go to cosmetology. I figured as that if I was in cosmetology I could keep my hair done and hang out with the old timers. Because I was a little tomboy some females thought that I was gay and I got letters constantly from them saying that they would take care of me and that they wanted to get with me. I was appalled to say the least and my answer was still the same, hell naw! All the correctional officers there took to me because I was the youngest female in the prison. So I basically got away with almost anything.

In the evening everyone would go to the dining room for recreation. At every table you had something going on. From playing spades for cigarettes, playing tunk, females and their lovers sitting in the cut fondling each other. You name it, it was done in there. About a month after I had been there, I got curious about the mating thing. This one particular girl kept trying to holla at me. So at the advice of my one of the old timers, I started kicking it with her. Rose was thirty and I was sixteen. She showed me a lot of attention, that I was starving for and my curiosity took over. One night while we were sitting in the rec room she tried to kiss me. I got angry because I thought all we were supposed to do is talk and shit. So when I got to my dorm I told the old timer and she was like "Shit go for it the bitch is going to take care of you!"

Everybody in the prison had a prison family and they were called your mom, state dad and so on and so forth. My state granddad was notorious and she got a lot of respect around the prison. So did her wife, Daisy. By them being popular anybody in their family was too.

After that incident Rose and I took it to another level. When her dad sent her money he sent me money too. Whatever she got at commissary I got half of. There also was this white girl named Donna who liked me also. Just to be up in my face she had to buy me tennis shoes, or whatever I wanted her to get. When I wasn't with Rose I was with my state family, or playing softball. Six months before my release date Rose wanted to know if we could have sex. Because I knew what that entailed, I told her "Bitch surely you don't think I'm getting ready to put my mouth on you?" She was like "No, It's all about you." Needless to say I had my first sexual encounter with a woman. To me it was just that, an encounter. I didn't see what all the excitement was about. I still felt nothing. I guess I wasn't really into it like that. After that day we were inseparable.

My release date was quickly coming up March 24, 1984. The closer it got the sadder Rose became. I promised her that I would keep in touch and holla at her once she got home. When I got home alot of things had changed. All the girls I use to hang out with were shooting dope and prostituting. I promised myself that whatever happened I wouldn't result to standing on a corner selling my body.

I went to stay with Ms. Bee, Carmelita and I was still tight to death. Junior had just gotten out of prison also, but he was in the church really hard. We never got back together, but I would see him years later. I got back into the grove boosting, hanging out. Ms. Bee ran a bootleg house so it was constantly something going on there. Around August of eighty four, I got a call saying that one of my mother brothers were in town with a guy from our neighborhood, Wayne. Wayne had been on the road playing the con game with my uncle. Once he learned how much money all my uncles were making he asked them to hip him to the game also. I have to say that I was a very promiscuous girl then, I actually thought that I could have sex with a guy and he would fall instantly in love with me. I also thought that I could be justified that way, but the only feelings I got out of sex is afterwards. I would feel like shit. Not to mention my self esteem was so low. I didn't think I was pretty, and I always thought I had to prove something to somebody. So I slept with Wayne.

I ended up going on the road with him and my uncle. They would stop in different towns playing the stuff a short con on people. We stopped over in New Orleans. While over there Wayne took me downtown bought me two or three outfits. Then that night while we were in our room he gave me a note pad with what I was supposed to say to a (lame) person when I stopped them. I told him I wasn't stopping no god damn body and to take me home. Wayne had been really nice to me the whole trip. Now, I knew the reason he wanted me to play the game and if I did as his woman I would have to give him my money.

"How could you just leave standing alone in a world that's go cold? The world is so cold! Maybe I'm just to demanding. Maybe I'm just like my father, too bold. Maybe I'm just like my mother she's never satisfied! This is what it sounds like when doves cry. Prince's song was playing on the radio as we were going back up I-59 to Birmingham. I wonder if Prince knew when he wrote that song that he was hitting home for a lot of people including myself.

We made it back to Birmingham. Wayne dropped me off at Ms. Bee's. About two or three days of being home I noticed my uncle and Carmelita had started kicking it real strong. Before I knew what was going on, Carmelita had started talking about she was going on the road with my uncle and Wayne. I couldn't let my partner out do me so I said I was going too. We were headed to Chicago. On the way Wayne and my uncle started hipping us to the game so that once we got to Chicago we'd know what to do. There were four types of con games the stuff, the drag, and the donation, and the police game. They turned us out to the drag because you could play for more money.

We finally made it to Chicago. We stayed in a hotel on Cicero called the Saratoga. At first, the only thing me Carmelita and I did was go with them while they worked. Then we started going out and working too. It's amazing as I think about whatever criminal acts hustlers committed they viewed it as a regular working job. Whenever we went out in the morning we called it work.

Freebasing was the in thing back then. People were mixing cocaine and baking soda together, cooking it up and smoking it. Some people called it rock; it would eventually be known as crack.

My uncle would send me up 79th and Halsted. I was suppose to meet this guy, give him the money then get the aluminum foil package for him. This had cocaine in it. Once I got back to the room he and Wayne would cook the cocaine up in this little glass tube mixed with baking soda to make the cocaine hard. After they did that they would put it on a pipe and light it with a cotton ball on the end of a clothes hanger sticking it in some 157 rum. They would hit (smoke) that pipe and the next thing you know they would be hiding behind couches telling me to be quiet. After a couple of days Carmelita asked if could she try it, she started tripping just like them.

As time progressed I would learn that cocaine had a different effect on people. One night I decided I would try some of this shit too. When I pulled on the pipe and inhaled my whole throat froze up, I could not catch my breath and thought that that was the worse feeling ever. I thought I was dying. I never tried it again with them after that night.

One day Wayne told me he wanted me to meet somebody. When he introduced us he told me that her name was Kim. So I'm still like "okay." I was known for violence so he was trying to see where my head was. After picking her up everyday going out to dinner, he told me this was my wife-in-law which meant that your man had more than one woman. I was really hurt, because again I thought that Wayne genuinely cared for me. Although, I vowed never to trust anybody, the first man to show me any attention, I would instantly fall in love, but I was determined not to let him know. I remember this one Friday night it was Wayne's birthday, and we had took a good piece of money. When we picked Kim up we didn't take her back home. So I'm thinking "I know this mother fucker don't think this bitch is fixing to get in the bed with us!" That's exactly what happened. We were drinking and free basing next thing I know we were all in the bed together, hand and mouths going everywhere. Before I knew it he had slipped out of the bed and there was no one in bed but me and her. It was like we were in a frenzy as angry as I was with him the sex was feeling good. She and I were having each other, but after the buzz wore off. I felt so degraded and I guess I just kept expecting different results. Praying for different results.

I stayed awake long after they had gone to sleep. I made up my mind I was going home because this shit was too deep for me. I got up, took me a shower, grabbed five hundred dollars off the dresser and took a cab to the greyhound bus station. I started noticing too that anytime things didn't go like I thought they should I would end up back where the drama originated from, home.

When I got home I started working at a barber shop downtown called Talk of the Town. Bro Jones was the owner and he believed in giving everyone a chance. He let me be the shampoo girl and make a little money. After a couple of days I noticed this pimp named Yogi checking me out through the window. Sometimes he would just come in so I could put activator in his gherri curl then give me a big tip. Bro Jones happened to notice Yogi paying me a lot of attention. He pulled me to the side one day and told me I shouldn't be affiliating with Yogi because was a pimp. Anytime a person told me I shouldn't. I felt that I should.

I started going out with Yogi, he would say little shit like "Ain't no money like ho money." I was like, "they don't ask you how you made it when you take it to the bank." I politely informed him that I was a thief and I wasn't going to sell no pussy point blank period. Like it really made any difference, because the money I made boosting I would give to him. Through the years I noticed that it was something about women with low self-esteem that attracted nothing ass niggas. We felt that we had to except anything as long as he said he was my man. As long as I was paying him he didn't matter how I got it either. I worked during the day and his other ho's worked at night. So when they went on the strip he would send me downtown to pick up the money from them. Those bitches were smoking hot too. What none of knew, is that Yogi really didn't give a fuck about any of us. He told us what we wanted to hear to get what he wanted to get. We were all the same to him, nothing.

Things were getting kind of hectic and I was falling for this nigga hard. If I didn't leave now, I wouldn't leave at all.

I called my mom and asked her if she'd send me the money for a bus ticket. She said yes, and I caught the bus the next day going to New York City.

Part 2

Volunteer

I T WAS TWENTY eight hours before we finally made it to New York. My mama told me when I got there not look up because if I looked up people would know I wasn't from New York and try to run game on me. My mama and my James picked me up from the Port Authority on 42nd Street. Once we got in the car they asked me a whole bunch of questions about what was going on in Birmingham. On our way uptown we stopped at a hotel called the Riverton on 132nd street and Lenox. My mama went upstairs and came back down. When she got in the car she opened her hand and showed me these little vials with red tops. She asked me had I ever smoked any. I told her yeah and she handed me three for myself. James looked at her and asked "Shawty why did you give her that?" she said "hell she do it anyway so why not?" I didn't want her to think that I was a square, and on top of that I would do anything if it was going to make me look good to her. I constantly needed her approval. You know, I wanted her to hug me, or just say she loved me. She never did so I had to except the little bit of attention I did get from her.

Once we got to their hotel which was on 145th and Lenox we went up to their room. Me coming to New York was just hog heaven for my mama and James. Because I knew how to play the game they didn't have to worry about getting a connection for work. After we smoked the crack I went to sleep, looking forward to the next day. I was so excited because now I and my mama could really get to hang out together.

The next day while they were coping their morning fix (heroin) they introduced me around to all the other hustlers. All of them were out buying drugs so that they could get well before going on to work.

After coping her heroine my mama and I went to work. We made about $1,500.

When we got back to the hotel James asked me where my money was. I told him he had me fucked up. "My mama is your woman not me!" Then I left. I went to a crack house on 117th and 7th avenue. It was set up like a bar only they served crack instead of liquor. I rented me a pipe and ordered ten dime rocks I smoked some there then I went and got me a room, bought the paraphernalia I needed and bought me something to eat. Then I chilled. When I got back to my mama's hotel all my clothes were sitting at the bottom of the steps. I went upstairs to ask my mama why was my clothes down there? James said "you're grown so go find you somewhere to stay" And I stood looking at this nigga like who in the fuck is he talking to? My mama was sitting in the room and didn't say a word. Then he slammed the door in my face. I was so goddamn mad. I picked up a folding chair in the hallway, knocked on the door, as soon as that nigga opened that door and stuck his head out. I bust that bitch dead in his hard ass face.

My mama came out the door grabbed me and told me, "If you hit him again I'll kill you!" Oh, my God! She should have just stuck me in my chest with a knife. All of the air left out of my body. I couldn't believe my mama said that to me. It shouldn't have been a surprise because she had always put that him before me and my sister. But it hurt just the same. I walked out of the hotel in a daze not knowing where I would go. I had enough money to get a room for a couple of days, but then I had caught a habit and didn't realize it. So it wasn't before long I was back on the streets. I didn't know my way around yet, except for the few places I had found on my own on 7th avenue. 7th avenue and 123rd street where most of the hustler's hung out at during the day. That's where I went hoping I'd see someone from home. Since I had that episode with my mama and James about work. I decided I wasn't going to play the con game. I had no idea where I was going; I didn't even know what I was going to do to survive.

I had heard a lot of people talking about this dude they called June Bug. I was warned to stay away from him because he was trifling and low-down, but I also gathered that a lot of these so called players were just straight scared of him. The streets were like women, they were always talking. I had heard that a dude name Blue Beard had slapped June Bug one night in a bar. June Bug, supposedly came back and shot and killed Blue Beard. While a lot of people feared him, they also despised him.

I was up on the corner trying to figure out what my next move would be, and who walks up? None other than June Bug. He had a lot of energy, he smiled a lot, and it was something about that smile that blew me away. I had the honor of having that smile turned to me. I looked over at him and our eyes clashed. My coochie was doing somersaults, and the fact that everyone kept saying stay away from June Bug drew me nearer. I would regret that decision over the years hundred times.

He looked over at me and said "Lord have mercy; look at Ms. Mary's granddaughter. I smiled. He walked over to me and asked if I remembered him. I told him no, that I didn't. He said, "Remember that day I was in your grandma's living room?" "Remember I asked you what your name was, and Ms. Mary told me none of my goddamn business?" The recognition came fast. I remember walking back through the front room and he said, "I'm gonna wait for you."

After we got reacquainted he asked if I wanted to take a walk with him. I asked him where we were going. He said, "King Base spot," which was a crack house on 122nd between 7th and 8th avenue. When we got upstairs into the apartment June Bug hollered at a few people then asked Vera, King Base's ugly ass girlfriend where King Base was. She said something smart then went in the back to get him. King base came out, him and June Bug kicked it for a minute, then pulled out a hundred dollars and told King Base to give him five fat twenties. He came back with the product, June Bug gave me two and he kept three. For the next couple of days I and he hit every crack house in Harlem.

After June Bug realized I had no intentions of playing the con game he started acting really cold towards me, then all of a sudden I started seeing his daughter's mother Cheryl up on the avenue. I was producing anything so he had to go to the female that was giving up the money. Back then, in our environment, the female that was giving up the most money was the top bitch.

June Bug started acting like I didn't exist and that really hurt. But I was to learn the cold hard way that it was called survival, it was nothing personal. I chalk that shit up like I had done everything else in my life, and kept it moving. I want up to the hotel where my mom was living we had started speaking again after that last episode. James wasn't there so I went on up. We sat and kicked it for a minute, and then my mom went to the bathroom, while she was in the bathroom I looked in the bible where she always kept her money. There was one hundred and seventy five dollars in there and I took it. My stomach started feeling like I had to go to the bathroom. That's the feeling you get when you're craving the crack. Instead of just taking ten or twenty dollars. I took it all. I left while my mom was in the bathroom. I caught a cab down to King Base's spot, and as soon as I hit that first rock I was in heaven. I realized that when I smoked crack I felt nothing, it made me forget about all the problems I had and I didn't have to worry about nothing or nobody.

I heard a loud banging at the door. I looked up. It was my mom. It was like she was going in slow motion. She was screaming at me. "Why did you take all my money?" Tears rolling down her face. She said "you didn't have to take all my money." I didn't know that my mom was a heroin addict and that she depended on that money to get her morning fix with. James grabbed her and was pulling her out the door. I just looked at her like she wasn't shit and kept smoking.

At that point I didn't give a fuck about nothing and nobody. I sat in that dope house for three days. No bath, no food just smoking. People would come in and offer me dope and I just sat there I couldn't move. It got so bad that my cycle had come on and the only time I went to use the bathroom was to stuff more tissue in my panties. Through the cloud in my head I kept hearing people say that something was stinking really bad. I had no idea it was me until one of my mama's friends (Beatnik) pulled me up out of there to take me somewhere so that I could bath, eat and get some rest. When I tell you I really didn't give a fuck no more. Please, believe me! I was tired, I was hurting; I was confused, I was lost and turned out.

I stayed at the Riverton hotel for three or four days. Beatnik's woman, Johnny Mae made sure I had clean clothes and ate. After I ate I went back out in the street.

See you have to understand "crack heads" perceived the world a whole other way from people that don't drugs at all. To me I didn't have a motherfucking problem. So after I got me a little rest, a bath, and some food. Shit, I jetted. All I wanted to do was get high. Then I started thinking which was dangerous than a motherfucker for myself and whoever else was around. I thought I might as well go ahead and play the game. At least I'll have some money and I could get me a room. The thing was I needed a connect. A con man wouldn't let a single female go to work with their woman unless the female had a man. That was the rule in the game, a man didn't do business with a woman, and you had to have a man. I had to choose a nigga to get a hook-up. I was walking and thinking so hard I didn't realize that I had walked up by King Base's place. As I'm going up the steps. I run into O and Michael Angelo. They were supposed to be big time pimps back in the day. And their women were known for taking large amounts of money with the "Drag" I guess pimping wasn't paying enough so they started playing the con game. I was told that years ago before the female could "Drag" they had to be hipped to the ho game first. Before I made it to the first landing O said, "Where are you going?" I said in return, "with you," I didn't know shit about this nigga. All I knew is that when a broad choose it would be all over the wire like the New York Times, and I definitely wanted June Bug to hear it out of sheer spitefulness. If I got into the car with O I was agreeing to be his broad, and what was understood didn't need no explaining.

I got in the car. O started asking me a bunch of questions. I was so tired that I just answered yes to everything. I didn't know that I was making a deal with the devil himself.

O lived in the Stadium Hotel. That's where a lot of other players lived also. On the way to the hotel, he let me know that he had a woman and her name was Resha. He told me that Resha would be okay with me staying there. In other words Resha would be my wife-in-law. It was cool with me because at this point I really didn't give a fuck one way or another. So much shit had gone on. What was the the worst that could happen?

We got on the elevator and went to the third floor. They stayed in room 306. O walked in the door with me behind. He introduced us to each other. They also had a little baby; she was only about 2 months old. Resha was a beautiful girl with a pretty smile; she made me feel at home. She asked me was I hungry. I told her no. I was just tired. So after I took a shower, I got into the bed and fell in a deep sleep. That was the most rest I had had in months. The next morning I was woke up by Resha. She asked me if I wanted to go to work. I said "yeah, but isn't today Sunday?" she said "yeah, but we were gong to play the stuff (short con) not drag." We ate breakfast; afterwards Resha gave me one of her outfits to put on. Before we left she asked me did I know how to play? If not, then she would tell me what to say. I assured her that I could. This was my initiation into there family.

Our destination was the Bronx on Fordham Road. There was always a lot of activity going on up there no matter what day it was. As soon as we got out of the car, the first lame (victim) Resha caught was the one we played, and we came off with $4,700. This was a good sting on a Sunday.

We were riding back to the hotel talking plenty of shit. As we're waiting on the elevator to come down. The doors opened, and O was getting off. He said "I thought I told you bitches to go to work!" We were like "we did" and showed him the sting. Him calling me a bitch didn't bother me. I had been called a bitch for so long that I forgot what my real name was. O told us to go to the room that he'd be right back. Of course on his way to wherever he was going he let it be known that you had two of the baddest young bitches in the country. When O came back he gave me and Slim, both money and crack cocaine. I asked him to get me another room because I didn't reel comfortable smoking around the baby. When I got in my room I showered, relaxed, and smoked crack. Throughout the evening Resha or O would come down and check on me. Then one time they came together he wanted to see me and Resha have sex with each other. We did. I felt nothing. I just wanted them to get out so I could smoke my dope. O came back down to the room later on and we were kicking it, all of a sudden he hit the pipe next thing I know this nigga has jumped in the shower fully dressed, screaming that he was on fire. After a while he calmed down got in the other bed and went to sleep. So I'm thinking to myself what kind of shit have I got myself caught up in? I got up, put on my clothes as quietly as possible, reached into O's pocket, took the money and left. I had no idea where I was going. I remembered this dope house on 126th that not too many people knew about. I took a cab there. Once, I got in there I noticed one of my James friend was in there. We sat down there and smoked crack nonstop for two days. After all the money was gone he left and I started weighing my options, it didn't look good.

I left there walking. I had no idea where I was going. I stopped at a phone booth and called my mama. She asked where I was and that O had been looking for me. Then I called the hotel and talked to Resha. She asked me where I was, and that O was mad as hell. She told me to come on back to the hotel, because if he caught me in the street that he would hurt me bad. I went back.

When I got to the room O was there. He looked at me and told Resha, "I'll be back. If I stay here I'm going to kill this bitch!" He left. Resha asked me why I left. I just looked at her. By the time I got out of the shower, I was so tired I could hardly stand up. I lay down and was asleep instantly.

In my sleep I heard a lot of noise I thought it was a dream until I opened my eyes and seen O standing over me. He hit me in the head with an aerosol can. I jumped up grabbed the baby hoping that he wouldn't hit me again. That didn't stop him. He took his pocket knife out and hit me on top of the head with it. All I could do is scream. He told me if I dropped his baby he would kill me. All the time was going on Resha was asking O to please let her get the baby. He turned on her and said, "Bitch you were down with it too!" He told us that we were responsible for each other and that if one of us fucked up then the other one would get it too. Soon after, he left us in the room. We were both shaking and crying, too scared to lie back down.

The next morning he told us to get ready for work. While I was in the shower Resha stuck her head in the door and said she was going downstairs, that she'll be right back. As I was putting my clothes on O came in the room and asked where Resha was I told him she went downstairs. After an hour or two had passed, O came back to the room and said "The bitch ran off with my baby." For three days straight we searched high and low for Resha. On the fourth day, O was disheveled, and hadn't shaved in a couple of days. I could tell that not seeing the baby was having a bad effect on him. He walked in the door and said, "I know where this bitch is at," I asked him if he wanted me to go with him he said no. About two or three hours later I heard a commotion in the hallway, the door flies open and it's Resha, the baby and O. Resha was crying and O was talking crazy. "Bitch did you think you could get away from me?" Come to find out this nigga named Pretty Steve had tried to holla at Resha. He told her that if she ever wanted to choose a real man then all she had to do was holla at him. And that's exactly what she did.

After a day or so when shit had calmed down a little Resha told me that O had kicked the door in at Pretty Steve's house, drug her and the baby out, and Pretty Steve ran.

We went to work the next morning and for some reason there was a black cloud hanging over us. We couldn't get any money at all. So I said, "fuck it" let's go back up town, and then we'll go back out tomorrow." When we got uptown to a 132nd and Lenox, I saw O coming out of McDonalds with this strange look on his face. He was looking at me, and he had tears in his eyes. Resha looked up she said, "Where's the baby?" He took his eyes off of my face, looked at Resha and said, "The baby's dead!" Resha almost lost her mind. I asked what happened; he said "The hospital said she died from crib death."

We went up to Harlem Hospital to see her. She was lying on a table, and she looked like a little angel. Resha was inconsolable. We were to have her funeral Saturday. We worked so that we could get the money to bury her. Neither one of us were up to dealing with people so we weren't able to get no money. Just so happen that Friday, Michael Angelo's woman had took a great deal of money he gave O two thousand dollars just on the strength of the game and were able to bury the baby peacefully. God had other plans for her.

After that things got worst. It seemed that baby girl's death had really taken a toll on them both. O was still jumping in showers and shit, paranoid as ever. Resha had started drinking. When ever we stayed at a hotel I always wanted my own room because when both of them got high together oh, my God! I wanted to get away from them and I didn't know how.

Eventually, the opportunity presented itself one early Monday morning. Resha and I had our own cars now, so we went to work with different people. That way if one of us didn't sting the other one would. I stopped in front of the Riverton to get out and talk to other drag broads. I remember when we first started out none of the older broads wanted to work with us because they said we were too young. But now you couldn't beat these bitches off with a stick because I and Resha were doing our thing, getting paid like slot machines. I was 19 and Resha was 21. Once we start getting paid everyone wanted a connect with Toni and Resha. O wasn't having it. He felt that we had been slighted back in the day so he got us connect with other broads that were coming from out of town, just to be spiteful.

While I was sitting there talking the police pulled up behind my car, and I knew once O found out he was going to fuck me up because he had told us about stopping on that corner in the mornings.

The officer asked whose car it was I told him mine. He asked for a driver's license and registration or insurance. I had neither. So he took me in and towed the car. As we're headed to the precinct, who did I see walking but June. I held my hands up to let him know that they were taking me to jail. He was running to catch up to the car. I guess he knew that they were taking me to the precinct on 8th avenue. They kept me there for about an hour then they let me go. When I walked outside June Bug was standing there. He said that one of the players had told him that I was charged with so he knew that they wouldn't keep me there that long. I still hadn't called O to tell him what had happened. As we were walking June Bug told me he heard about the sting I took when I first got with O, and about the money me and Resha were taking, and lying talking about he missed me and shit. He could have saved that spiel for someone else. All he had to do was say come on, and I was coming. I was sick of O.

June Bug, finally got around to saying, "are you ready to come back home now?" I said "yes, but what about O?" He said, "Let me handle O. June Bug said we were going up to the Riverton. If I told you I wasn't scared I'd be telling a damn lie! I knew how ignorant O was, but also knew June Bug was a damn fool too, but he played by the rules. If I chose June Bug, O couldn't do nothing but respect it. We were on the first floor of the hotel and all of a sudden I heard O's voice "Where's that bitch at?" June Bug responded "she's with me." Resha was standing behind O saying "come on Toni." I just shook my head and let June Bug handle it from there.

From that point on June Bug and I was the Bonnie Clyde of Harlem. Neither one of us gave a fuck about nothing. I don't know if we even cared about each other! If June Bug slapped a nigga, I slapped their bitch. Whatever he was down for so was I. Even though my mind was distorted with drugs, if I was down with you, you had a good soldier.

Around September, I was getting money fast and June Bug was popping his collar. He was bragging to the other players that his broad came up town no later than 12:00 p.m. That was a good thing in the game because it meant that I was handling my business. The only rules June Bug had was for me to come straight home after work and not to stop at the crack spot. The only problem I had with June Bug was his stupid ass baby mama, Cee. Even though she played the game too, she constantly threatened him with the police. Cee would often take stings and June Bug would go be with her for a day or two, but before he left he would always leave money and dope for me. A lot of times he wouldn't stay gone that long because he was too worried about what I was doing while he was gone. I remember this one weekend he was gone. Jewel asked me if I would play the stuff with her. Jewel was an older drag broad that use to work with my mother. I told her yes, she told me before we went downtown she had a stop to make. We stopped at a hotel on 148th, when we got up there these two older players were up there Glasses and Saul. Rumor had it that they had taken at least $12,000 grand that day. Glasses didn't know who I was or who I was with because he started talking to Saul and Jewel as if I wasn't even in the room. After a while Saul and Jewel said they were going to the store. Glasses started talking about how pretty I was. All I wanted to know was where this trick had hid the money and I was going to burn his ass up.

Finally, I said "Let's go get another room; I'm scared June Bug might find us here." We left and went to this hotel called the, Dawn. I heard that Glasses had a sleeping disease so I was counting on that to help me out too.

TONI SHEALEY

Once we got in the room. He handed me a hundred dollar bill to go up on 148th and Amsterdam to get ten rocks. As we were smoking he wanted me to walk around naked. He was like fifty-six, if that's what floated his boat, oh well. That's what I was going to do. Whatever I did, I had to hurry up and do it quick.

Around the sixth time he sent me to get crack, I seen where he had the money. Instead of going to 148th I went to 132nd and Lenox. When I got there June Bug was standing on the corner furious. I jumped out of the cab and before he could start going off I told him that Glasses didn't know that I had been hip to the game. All he knew is that I was June Bug's woman. He had a beef with June Bug from back in the day and he was going to use me as revenge. I told him that I went along with it as if I didn't know any better, then I seen where he hid his money and came to find him.

He said we were going to catch a cab and go back to the hotel. The whole time we were riding back he had this crazy ass look in his eyes, and he kept saying over and over "is this how this nigga want to play? Before we got there he gave me instructions on what to do. I knocked on the door. Glasses said, "Who is it?" I said, "Toni" he opened the door and June Bug kicked it in the rest of the way. He grabbed Glasses and said to me, "bitch get the money." I got the money and ran to the door. Glasses tried to stop me, but June Bug was still tussling with him. We made it down stairs and told the man to please buzz the door. He wouldn't so June Bug kicked the whole glass out of the door. Fortunately for us a cab pulled up. When I looked out of the back window, Glasses was running behind the cab butt ass naked, screaming "they got my money" After that incident we always had to watch our backs cause Glasses sometimes went to some of the spots we went to.

June Bug went to prison in November of 84. I was so depressed. I smoked crack all the way through Christmas and New Years, 1984 and didn't know it had come and gone. Those niggas that called themselves players wouldn't fuck with me because although they knew my nigga was locked up they were scared to fuck with me because they knew he would not be gone long. On top of that they knew I was just as dirty, low down and trifling as he was. I got me a room and all I did was go to work when I could get a connect; buy me food, cigarettes and crack and just straight trip by myself.

I had a Sugar Daddy that owned an arcade on Lenox between 132nd and 131st. Norman was good to me; whenever I needed money I would holla at him. We would go to a hotel way out in Long Island or near Belmont Race Track, he loved to gamble. As the days and months went by I lost a lot of weight. Now food wasn't even important anymore. I worked to get high. James even tried to talking to me; I didn't want to hear that shit. Crack was the only thing that made me feel good, it didn't hurt me, and it didn't let me down.

Finally around December 1985, Wayne came into town, he and Kim my James told him where I was and that I had lost my damn mind. When, the knock came; I was sitting in the room in the dark. I opened the door Wayne looked at me and there were tears in his eyes. He said, "I didn't turn you out like this!" He told me to get my things that I was going home to Birmingham. You would have thought Jesus Christ was standing there himself. I was so tired and weary and I just collapsed in his arms. He took me over to the hotel him and Kim were staying at in New Jersey. She looked at me like what is that bitch doing here. I just walked past her, took me a shower and got in the bed. But before I lay down I told her, "I would never let a bitch know that they intimidated me." "Besides I don't want your man." From that point on we had an understanding.

The week before Christmas. I told Wayne I wanted to be home by Christmas to see my sister. We traveled through Ohio, Pittsburgh, and several other states. We made it to Birmingham, December, 24.

By this time Trice was 15 and a young lady. I hadn't seen her in almost four years. I had gained some weight back. I was glad because I didn't want her to see me in the condition I had been in. I stayed at my grandmas house, that pervert was still there. He eased around me anytime we happened to be in the same room. I was big enough to defend myself now. That coward wouldn't dare say anything to me. I hung out there for awhile so I could be with my sister.

My mama baby brother and I were really close; I guess it was because we were so close in age. He was more like my brother than my uncle. One night me, my uncle and Trice, a few other friends were sitting in the kitchen just kicking it. This guy was standing by the refrigerator and he was saying something, whatever it was he was annoying me. I asked my uncle "Who is that?" He said, "That's Chucky from Collegeville." When it dawned on me what he had said. I looked up and it all came rushing back to me. When I was a little girl I had such a big ass crush on this boy. I said I was going to marry him when I got big. Chucky and Pee were really good friends growing up. Every time Chucky came around I would sit and stare at him for hours. I thought he was the finest boy ever. From that night forth we were inseparable, and a week from New Year's 1986. Chuckie asked me to marry him. My track record with guys hadn't been good, but I thought if I got married things would be different this time. He loved me, didn't he?

We were married January 25, 1986. The first mistake I made is letting him talk me into staying at his mom's house until we found somewhere to stay. Chucky worked at a steel plant Metal Products. He got paid every Friday and his mom usually got the check. He was a married man now so the wife got the check, right? On top of that his ghetto fabulous ass baby's mama called the house every five minutes to let me know that she was his baby's mama. I was like "So I'm his wife" I had started going to college anywhere to get the fuck up out of that house. I worked for this little telemarketing place in the mall part time. I was really trying to do the house wife thing I really was.

One Sunday on our way to church my mom called me from Philadelphia to tell me that my Pee had been diagnosed with A.I.D.S. Back then people were really ignorant about the facts concerning HIV. Everyone was devastated. In spite of the things in the past I still felt a loss. I felt like everything was closing in on me and I needed to get away. My partner, Tammi and I, decided that we would go on the road. I had started playing the game again a month after Chucky and I were married. Money wasn't coming in fast enough, I had got that itch again, I was bored and her man was locked up in California, and to top it off I had started smoking crack again.

Four months after I was married, I left my husband. Tammi and I went from state to state heading west. One stop was in Shreveport Louisiana. We decided if we got enough money there we wouldn't go on back to Birmingham. The third day there we got arrested. After about three months of going back to court the judge finally released us and gave us a floater out of Louisiana with the conditions that we not come back. They only had to tell me once. When we got home I didn't want to see Chucky so I called his mother. I asked if Chucky was home, if not then I was coming to get my clothes. Well while she was packing my clothes he came in and asked her why she was. She told him that I was at my grandma's house and I wanted my things. Needless to say, he came to Norwood and when I seen him on that porch he looked like something from Tales from the Crips. Chucky had started smoking crack. I tried to mask my disgust. I asked him why he didn't bring my clothes. He claimed that he was so excited to see me that he forgot. After a few minutes I was able to talk him into going back and getting them. Really, just to get him out of the house because, I needed to get away from him.

When he left I made a call to this guy that I met in jail in Louisiana. His name was Texas, and that's all I ever knew. He told me while we were in jail that if I ever wanted to hook up with a real nigga to holla. I told him that I was tired of Birmingham. At the time him, his homey, Stepdown and his broad Jada were out in Arizona hustling. He said if I really wanted to come he would go to the airport and purchase the ticket for the next day, which was on Friday.

Chucky wouldn't leave my side. He stayed with me at my grandma's house, until the next morning. We got up around 5:30 a.m. Chucky had to be at work at 7:00 am. As soon as he left I started packing my shit. My plane was to leave at nine. Tammi called me and asked me if I was sure I wanted to do this because I really didn't know anything about Texas and she was really worried about me. I told her I had to go. That I couldn't stay around. I was a very impulsive person. I was like a caged animal if you backed me in a corner I came out fighting. I didn't know how to deal with problems so I'd just run.

I caught my flight and I changed planes in Dallas/Fort Worth airport. Once I got to Phenoix, I looked around and I saw Texas standing at the gate. I knew how he looked because I had passed him numerous times going to the doctor and we talked through the window everyday. This nigga could have been Jeffery Dalmer, Hannibal Lector, anybody. I just didn't give a fuck! The three months that we talked in jail I found out that he was from Dallas, Texas and that he played the game also. I told him things about me and in one of our conversations, the topic of shooting dope came up. I told him I detested heroin users. I guess because my mama did it. I couldn't stand the sight of needles.

We ended up at our hotel. We ate drank, took pictures I could send to Tammi, and for the next two days we just righteously got to know each other. On the third day this nigga turned into Jeckle and Hyde. When I woke up Texas was in the bathroom throwing up. I asked him if I could help, or maybe get some Pepto Bismo. He said "no" he'd be fine. I got up went out and got breakfast. This nigga was happy, singing and shit. My warning bells should have gone off then. The next morning the same shit happened so instead of me saying anything I just went to get our food. Once I got out the door I realized that I had left the money on the bathroom counter. I reached over to get the money and I turned my head to the left Texas was sitting on the toilet with his arm tied and a needle sticking out of his arm nodding. I thought "what the fuck have I gotten myself into?" Texas looked up and seen me standing in the door he was like "hey baby." Now all I could think about was how was I going to get away from this nigga? I didn't have any money and he followed me around everywhere. At the time they were playing the donation and I hadn't been hipped to that yet. He didn't care it seemed as if I was dealing with a new person than what I started out with. I told him I didn't know how to play the donation, he was like "bitch you gone learn" I had jumped out of the kettle into the frying pan.

The four of us traveled from Pheonix to Tuscan then to L.A. We took a little money on the way. Just barely enough to get their drugs and a room. I remember one day we were at the service station. Texas got out to pay and pump the gas. When he got back in the car he slapped me and said that when he got out we talked, but when he got back in we stopped talking. I could not believe this shit. Then another time we were driving and I had just gotten off the phone with my grandmama. This nigga said I called another dude. So he took both of his thumbs and tried to poke my eyes out. Well I guess Stepdown and Jada had had enough. Stepdown told Texas once we got to San Francisco he was going to have to dip. He said he didn't want Texas jumping on me in his car and, also because he had to see his parole officer. Stepdown took us across the bridge to Oakland. We got a hotel room and they left. I was alone with this goddamn fool. I had been surviving all my life, and it always seems that I had to get myself out of bullshit constantly. Somehow I would work this out.

This nigga had started shooting dope on a regular basis. He didn't give a fuck that it bothered me. Then in the hotel we stayed in I met this dude named Shorty Ken, he sold crack. Of course I started back using. I had to; this was the only thing that could help me black out this foolishness that I had gotten myself into.

We worked around downtown Oakland getting money. Plus Texas had a friend over in Berkley that he knew. One morning we were downtown and I noticed the lady working over in the jewelry store kept staring while we were playing this man. I didn't really pay too much attention to it. Until I looked up and the police as walking up to the table. They asked the man what did we tell him, and he told them. The officer explained to him that we were pigeon droppers (flim flammers), and that we were flim flaming him out of his money. I was taken to juvenile because I told them I was 16. Texas went to jail. Once I got to the detention center. I realized that they intended on keeping me awhile so I told them my real age which was 21. They called my mom in Philly so she could verify what I told them. She sent me a bus ticket and they dropped me off at the greyhound bus station.

My conscience was really bothering me so I said let me see if I could find Texas to let him know that I was leaving. I could use the ticket any time long as the bus was going to Philly.

I checked the hotel they told me he had been there but left. Then I went down to his friend's house on Berkley and that's where he was. I hugged him then I told him that my mom sent me a ticket and I was going to Philly. He looked at me with so much hate in his eyes and he punched me, and then slapped me in my face. Cars were coming from each direction. I just ran in the middle of the street the people in the cars were blowing at me. I was crying because I didn't know which way to go. Texas was running behind me trying to catch me but I kept dodging behind the car. He kept saying "Lil mama let me talk to you." I said, "I don't want to talk, leave me alone!" He asked me "would you do me a favor and go take a sting with me, so I can have some money to get home?" I said "If I do will you leave me alone?" He said "Yes". So we ended up taking the DART (subway) over to San Francisco and because a lot of military men usually travel through there we decided to go to the bus station and also mostly because they carry a lot of cash. As soon as we got to the station a bus was unloading, the second passenger got off was a white guy coming from the army on leave. I cut into him to tell my story. Then I motioned for Texas to come in. We played that dude down to the switch. When I got ready to switch he grabbed my hand. I kicked him in the groin and threw the knot to Texas. Both of us took off running. It's a rule of the game if you get separated always go to the bus station we'll meet up there. I went back to the bus station in Oakland, and as far as I was concerned I had did my part. All I wanted to do was catch my bus.

About an hour after I got to the station. Texas pulled up in a yellow cab. He signaled for me to come here. I told him no to go on. He said "would you please come out to the cab for a minute?" When I got out there he was counting hundred dollar bills. I was like "Where did this come from?" He said, "The sting." Then he tried to give me some. I was like "no" you go ahead.

I caught my bus that night and I've never seen or heard from Texas again. It took the bus five days to get to Philly. We went through towns like Reno, Salt Lake City, Utah. I also had time to think about the situation I was on my way to. My mama was with this man named Doc. They hooked up when she got out of prison in Bedford Hills, New York. I had never really known Doc but I had dated one of his sons briefly in New York.

When we finally pulled into Philly I got off the bus looking for my mom, some guy walked up to me and asked me a question. I hate for strange men to talk to me so I turned my back to ignore him. Then he touched my shoulder and called my name. I turned around and said "who the fuck is you?" and why did you put your damn hands on me?" I heard my mama laugh as she came from around ole boy. She told me that the dude was Theo. Doc's oldest son. When I really looked at him I saw the resemblance. I caught my mama up on what had happened in California. She told me when I get some money I need to pay Doc back because he was the one that bought the bus ticket.

They lived on Tasker Street, nice neighborhood on the southside of Philly, over the top of a bar. My moms and Doc road over to New York every weekend. As far as I knew my mom wasn't using at this time. Once Doc came home and he told me what his rules were in his house. That shit went in one ear out the other. Because I only planned on being there as long as I could get some money and go back to New York. I chose Theo so Doc would let my mama work with me. Theo was a good looking dude; homeboy was just weak as hell. He let his dad talk to him like a straight punk.

Since I had been through all the sexual abuse and rapes having sex was boring to me. If a nigga knew the kind of shit going through my mind at the time his dick would have shriveled up. Because my little mind had been distorted when I was younger it gave me a fucked up perception of men. I felt that my pussy was a weapon and I could use it to get what I wanted out of them. Only thing I felt afterwards was shame, unattractive and sad. My heart was so empty. I had actually given up on being happy, I hadn't so far. My mom and I started working together and we were getting paid around that town. I had started building my jewelry wardrobe up. It was amazing having all these material things. I was still unhappy and lonely Theo would take me out to nice restaurants, shopping the whole nine. I just wasn't feeling ole boy so it wouldn't be long before he was history I forgot to mention if I had sex with a nigga I lost interest in them afterward. So I didn't need them to stay around to make me feel worse than I already was.

One night my mom and I went out to the mall. I wanted to go in this big store in Philly called Warnamakers because they had really pretty expensive things in there. On our way to the mall my mom stopped and bought some crack and that beast was unleashed in me again. See my mom didn't know how to be maternal she thought if me and her worked together, got high together we were bonding. I ended up smoking some crack that night. Before long Theo started smoking with us. One night my mama gave me and Theo a hundred dollars to go cope for her. We went and smoked that money up and when we got back we told her we had lost it. The last straw was when I told Theo to go get the box of change from up under his dad's bed. It was three hundred dollars in there and we took it.

Later on that evening Doc realized it was gone. He started going off on my mama. Then he told her "That bitch got to go." I told that motherfucker "That's your bitch, not me!" "Fuck you nigga I ain't got to stay here." So back to the bus station I headed, to New York City this time. Theo told me once I got there to call his brother and he'll come pick me up. My mind was already made up. I was going to the Riverton. I had heard June Bug was out, and although my mind was telling me, no, my feet were leading to the Riverton. I felt that June Bug was the only nigga that understood me, and definitely the only nigga that could handle me.

I went up to the Riverton. I ran into Reggie first. June Bug younger Brother. As soon as he seen me he was like "There go my sister-in-law." All the time that nigga was hoping I had some money so I could buy him a rock. I paid the lady at the desk for a room, put my things in there and headed up stairs to the second floor to buy me some dope. I told Reggie not to let June Bug know that I was in the hotel yet. Shit that was just like telling the town cryer not to yell. About ten minutes had passed next thing I know I hear "Where Ralph at?" Ralph was the nickname that he gave me.

He said, "Ralph you've been up here all this time and ain't looked for me?"

It was known that regardless if you were June Bug's friend or foe every one knew not to call themselves being with me. If they did they had made an enemy out of him. He felt that I belonged to him. And if I was with someone once he got out of prison I got back with him, because eventually one way or another it was going to be a problem for me and whoever I chose.

We went down to the room and he asked me where I had been, how I got back and a whole bunch of endless questions. We stayed up and smoked crack all night.

The next morning Theo's brother came down to the hotel calling up to me from outside. June Bug stuck his head out the window and told him to tell Theo I was back at home. I felt kind of bad so I slipped away to call Theo to tell him that as soon as I could take a sting I would come back to Philly and we'd get a place to stay. That was just a bargaining chip for him not to come over to New York because I knew it was going to be trouble if he did.

The next day June Bug got me a connect and I went to work. When I came back from work Theo was standing in the Riverton door way. I almost shitted on myself. I stood there, frozen in my tracks. June Bug walked up and looked in the direction I was looking in. He had my hand

and I felt when he tensed up. We continued into the hotel Theo stepped out of the way. I prayed that he didn't say anything to me. I exhaled as I got to the top of the steps. As we continued up to the second floor. I went in the room with Resha, she and O had moved into the Riverton. June Bug went on up to the third floor. Resha and I are sitting in the room kicking it and smoking, next thing I know Theo was coming up the steps and June Bug was going down the steps. The door was open to the room like it always is during the day. Theo called my name as soon as he got to the top of the steps June Bug pulled out a knife and started slicing at Theo. Theo ran back down the stairs, June Bug turned around and looked at me and said, "Bitch you called that nigga up here didn't you." Before I could get a word out that nigga had picked up a two by four and bust me I my head. That's the last thing I remembered before I blacked out.

When I woke up Resha was crying and saying, "Toni please wake up. June Bug was standing on the side of me with the pipe he told Resha to move over. He said "here Ralph hit this," I sat straight up in the bed. He told Resha "I told you that would get her up." I asked Resha what happened she told me Theo ran out of the hotel, and that she told June Bug what happened but hell it was too late then.

For the next couple of months everything remained the same except now was I so hooked on crack it was sad. In order for me to get up in the morning I needed crack. For me to go to bed at night I needed crack. June Bug knew this and that's how he controlled me.

I even set up two dope boys for him to rob. Whatever it took for me to get some crack that's what I did. I lived to get high, and I got high to live. The killing part about it half of these boys knew June Bug had ganked them, but they act as if they didn't to keep down confusion.

In November of 1986 June Bug went back to prison and I was out there on my own once again. Nobody bothered me though because they knew the rules still applied. I was still June Bug's girl ride or die.

I caught a case in January of1987 in Westchester County at Yonkers Race Track. I was given 1 ½ to 3 and sent to Bedford Hills Prison. Which was a reception area for anyone with 5 to 15 years or less. Anything higher than that you were at home. Once you got to Bedford you went through all lands of physical test to make sure you didn't have any communicable disease. After all the tests were done, which took about a week you were moved to population. Everybody knew each other because the majority of us came from Rikers Island or had hustled together at some point. Since I didn't have any family or support in New York I had to make sure I had. So the object was to find a female that was paid and that would take care of me. At that time I don't think I even had a sexual preference. I just went with the flow.

I had never seen as many females in my life with HIV until I got to Bedford. By me being ignorant of the disease, every time someone came near me I'd flinch or jump. Homosexual activity was a common thing, it was nothing to walk in the bathroom and see mates having sex, or walk past a bleacher on the yard and see them kissing. Bedford Hills also housed some pretty notorious people, hell I thought I was in Hollywood. For the three weeks I was there. I just was taking in the scene. After the three weeks I was shipped to Albion another female facility which was in upstate New York. It was much cleaner and stricter up there. I stayed there 6 months and then I was transferred to Bayview which was in Downtown New York. I applied for the drug program and was moved to the 8th floor in a much stricter environment than regular population. After a few weeks of being there I became involved with this female named Wisdom. She had been locked up since 1977 and this was 1987.

I obtained my G.E.D. took business classes and worked in the Department of Motor Vehicles call center while I was there. After a year I was released in June 1988. I was supposed to go to a halfway house, but I reported to my parole officer then I headed up town. Of course I went straight to the Riverton. I was out. I was looking good. People were acting as if they were glad to see me. They weren't doing nothing but stunting. Out of sight, out of mind. June Bug was still in prison so I was solo until I could find something to get into.

Later on that day one of my friends told me "Sonny Boy is upstairs" I said who in the fuck is Sonny Boy? She kept trying to describe him to me, until I just said fuck it let me go see who she's talking about. Once I got upstairs and seen him the recognition came fast. He noticed that I was standing in the door. Sonny Boy was an older, well dressed, small time drug dealer. He sold crack out of the hotel.

After awhile of me standing there he asked me if I wanted to go have lunch with him. I said yeah! After he made his transaction we went to Sylvia's, a soul food restaurant on Lenox 124th. We talked about me just getting out and of course he wanted to holla at me. We agreed that I'd stay with him hell I had nowhere else to go and to me it was all about survival. He had an apartment on 131st between Lenox and 5th. Sonny Boy was much older than I but he didn't look his forty four.

I moved what little stuff I had into his place. He was really good to me. Anything I wanted he got if for me. Eventually, I started getting restless, and me knowing he sold crack, and that he had it in the house had me crazy. I started going back to work. My first time out me and my connect stung for eight gees. Sonny Boy hadn't never had a female pay him so of course he was in heaven. I started hanging around at the Riverton and he would snap. Telling me I needed to go downtown, shopping, anything just don't hang around here. I guess he knew it was just a matter of time before I started smoking.

I had been living there almost a month and noticed that Sonny Boy hadn't asked me to have sex with him. In my mind I thought that was all men wanted. I started to think that he was gay or something. I asked him what the problem was. He told me that he found me very attractive but he didn't want me to think that all he wanted to do was have sex. That night, we did do it. I got pregnant with my son. Once he found out I was pregnant, he told me that I needed to make arrangements to go to Birmingham to have the baby. He even called my grandmamma, I assured him that as soon as I started showing I would leave.

Needless to say by this time I had started back smoking, and crack was plentiful. The thought of me going down south was ridiculous. One day he caught me coming from buying crack, he was like if you're going to smoke it you need to smoke it at home. Then I bought some crack from this rival drug guy. He couldn't wait to tell Sonny Boy.

This particular morning he had given me a hundred dollars before he left to go out. I smoked that up in less than an hour. I was an extremist. Always had to have a lot. Little did I know a person truly only gets high the first time that they smoke crack. After that you're just chasing a dream.

I don't know why, but all I knew is that I had to stay high. The world, as I knew it was fucked up. I felt that if I could stay high I wouldn't have to deal with shit. Later on that day I asked him for some more money he told me, "I gave you money already, so go home" I said, "How are you going to issue my money out to me?" Then I went to thinking this nigga think I'm something to play with. I'll show his ass! I went back around to the house and I tried to figure out where he would hide the money. While I was looking I was smoking too. I smelled smoke but I thought it was the smoke coming from my pipe. The dude next door to us knocked on the door and said, "Toni the house is on fire!" I said okay, but then the paranoia set in and I thought the guy was trying to come in rob me. I finally realized the house was really on fire, so I jumped out the window from the second floor. It's a wonder I didn't miscarry.

Today as I think back, God was determined for Wllie to be in this world. Because no matter what I did my baby held on till his time. We found out later on that it was the apartment on the first floor. It was later on that night before everything got back in order. I was still home by myself and was determined now more than ever to find some money or dope. I looked in his shoes up under the table and it was about an eight ball of crack in there and a roll of money.

I never liked getting high by myself so I went around a spot and Theo's brother was inside I told him to come and ride with me. We went and got a room on 135th and 8th. When we got in the room I told him what I had done. We stayed in that room to sun-up smoking crack. Neither one of us had been to sleep. When it dawned on me what I had really done, I told Theo's brother "We need to make this money back." When I was using it never dawned on me the seriousness of any situation until after it was over, and by then the damage would have already been done.

He was cool with it. So we went downtown to play the stuff. We stung then caught a cab back uptown. We got out on 127th and 7th.

Country, June Bug's half brother pulled up on the side of me in his car. He said, "That nigga is looking for you." I said, "Fuck Sonny Boy." He said "Not Sonny Boy, June Bug." County told me that he had gotten out today. I wasn't even concerned with Sonny Boy anymore. My dilemma was facing June Bug, and telling him I was pregnant.

The whole time we were together he had been trying to get me pregnant. Like we really needed to bring a child up in this madness. I cut Theo's brother loose. Then I went and got me another room. I guess I was trying to figure out how to approach him. I was never one to duck I just handled shit as it came, and I'd think about the consequences and repercussions later. I took me another shower, put my clothes on and decided to walk downtown from 145th to 132nd to the Riverton. I needed time to clear my head because I knew it was going to be a lot of drama.

I was sure this is where I'd find him. I was also pissed off because I was going to have to face this shit on my own. A lot of dudes feared June Bug and Sonny Boy was one of them.

I was thinking so hard I didn't realize that I was in front of the hotel. I felt like I was going in front of the firing squad. Finally, I went up the steps and ran into Reggie again. I believe this nigga had radar or something cause every time I came to the hotel he would jump out. This time he when hollered for June Bug he came out of a room from the left like he had been waiting for me. He hugged me then he said "Hey Ralph". I said, "I'm pregnant," he said, "Okay." From that point on my life became a living hell. Sonnyboy's scary ass wouldn't even come in the hotel because he thought June Bug was going to whip his ass. Every chance June Bug got he would straight dog Sonny Boy out and Sonny Boy acted as if I didn't even exist.

We got a room permanently in the hotel and we got high everyday from sun up to sun down. June Bug made sure he had crack for me every day before I went to work. It's the only thing that motivated me. I think he also knew that he had to keep me high, because I had a very rebellious spirit.

He had become so paranoid that if I went to the bathroom and stay too long he would jump on me. I remember one day sitting in the room singing the song "Thanks for My Child" by Cheryl Pepsi Riley and June Bug came in the room, punched me in my face. He was screaming. "Thanks for your child bitch?" "Thanks for your child?" Steadily beating me. I didn't understand why he was so angry. I just balled up on the floor and cried.

I was about 2 months along then. One of our friends ran in the room and jumped in front of me as he swung the broom it hit her instead of me. He pushed her down, picked up a television and threw it at my stomach. He was like "bitch I'm fixing to go, but you better try to find away to have an abortion." When I thought he was gone I walked out of the hotel, to use the pay phone by McDonalds. On my way out the door Country gave me twenty dollars and told me to go see about myself. I was so hurt mentally and physically. There was no one to turn to, no one to talk to because no one wanted to be involved. I tried calling Harlem Hospital to ask the lady about an abortion. I was crying so hard she couldn't even understand what I was saying. As I was walking towards the hospital a car passed and the Whispers song "Lost and Turned Out was playing. I felt just like the girl in their song, Olivia.

Once I got to the hospital, I told them I fell, so they wouldn't ask me so many questions. After I got checked out the nurse told me the baby was fine, but I needed to be more careful. It never once crossed my mind to go home to Birmingham because June Bug had scared me half to death, my self-esteem was very low, and I had no confidence in my self. June Bug had me believing that I couldn't make it without him.

I went to the pay phone and called up to the hotel. The lady at the desk asked me where I was, and that June Bug was worried about me. I took my dumb ass right on back over there. When I got upstairs he hugged me, told me he was sorry. Then he pulled the pipe out put the crack on it and said "look what I got for you."

We had many more instances like this every time we got high and he thought about me being pregnant. This one particular night I kept having really bad vibes. I had been to work, we had money, and June Bug was hanging out with Pinky this little dope kid. They had robbed this dude from Chicago, and came back in the hotel like every thing was cool. I told June Bug "please let's go get another room somewhere else. "He said no". Eventually, I fell asleep. When I woke up June Bug was standing over me with handcuffs on, and there was a detective in there also. June Bug looked at me and in my mind I was like "Thank God." Because I was so tired of him beating me.

As soon as scary ass Sonny Boy found out that June Bug was in jail he started bringing his sorry ass back around. My respect for him had gone down a notch after he didn't stand up to June Bug.

I started working with this older female from the Bronx; she would buy work from The Chicago, Boston and D.C. boys, and have it hooked up. Then we would go to Atlantic City to the casino's and get cash advances off of the credit cards. I was enjoying my freedom. I didn't have to answer to anybody, spent my money like I wanted to. I sent June Bug money and clothes over to Riker's Island one or two times. After that I didn't fell like I owed his ass a damn thing. I moved to a room up on the second floor after a while I started showing. All of the other dope boys in the hotel always looked out for me because when I had credit cards I'd always shop for them and buy the up to date shit.

About a week after being upstairs. I started noticing this dude come in and cop every day at the same time. He would always speak to me and I back. After a while he would stop hold conversations with me, and then he started calling me his little sister. His name was Sly and I thought he was fine as hell. Once we righteously started hanging, he told me he was from Brooklyn and he heard that I was a writer. He wanted to know if he got some work would I write it for him. Some times as he passed my door he'd throw me a different designer wallet that he'd took that day. As the days progressed it just seemed normal that we were in each others company. Sonny Boy didn't like that worth a damn. He would go off and say "Why every time I come around that nigga is around you?" I was like "That's my friend, that boy is like a brother to me." He kept on saying "That nigga wants you." I was sick of hearing it so I said "Yeah, whatever." I guess both of us were in a denial about our feelings for each other because one night it came to a head. One minute we were talking. The next minute we were all over each other.

When Sonny Boy came around to the hotel the next morning I said, "Don't come in here!" He said, "Why?" I said because "My man is in here."

You should have seen the shock on this face. Needless to say I had just ended up with another damn fool. Sly used heroin as well as crack so we always had to make sure we had money in the morning so he could get well. A lot of times he would try to keep up with me smoking, and have to sniff more heroin. My connect stop giving me work because she said my man was pick pocket so he should supply me with work. For some reason didn't too many people around the hotel care for Sly. I would find out soon enough.

If I had a good set of work I wanted like to go work it during the morning. Well, he only worked the 11:00 p.m. tip. That's when all the Broadway plays and musicals let out. So if he beat them that night the work probably wouldn't be good in the morning cause the vic would have called and cancelled there credit cards. This became a constant argument with him and me. It was like he didn't want me to get no money and on top of that he was obsessed with June Bug. He had heard how I was with June Bug so he wanted me to be that way with him. Sly had started beating me a lot to saying shit like "Bitch if June Bug were here you'd do it." It never occurred to me to leave because I felt that whatever was going on was what I deserved.

I got word through the grapevine that June Bug called and he wanted to know if I wanted that nigga handled. I told them to tell him no. I had gotten myself into this shit so I had to get myself out of it. With both of us smoking crack and him sniffing heroin we needed money constantly. Which wouldn't have been a problem if he had of worked with me. I always had to wait till he stung to get me some money and he definitely wasn't letting me go to work with no one else. Most time the wallets had money and he'd throw the credit cards away just so I couldn't work them. People started seeing how he was treating me, even the dope kids was like "What's up Toni?" "You need us to handle this?" I would always say no.

Things were rapidly getting out of hand. He had even robbed my connects son for dope. Every hotel we went to uptown wouldn't let us in because when this nigga got high he would tear the whole room up. Word got out to me again that I could come to the Riverton, but if Sly showed up his ass was history. I was eight months pregnant, my nerves were shot and I found out he was shooting the dope instead of sniffing. I was about to have a nervous breakdown.

I remember one evening we walked the streets all night. We even went to Brooklyn to his mom's house and she didn't even want him there. We ended up sleeping in the subway. February 25, 1989 two days before my due date. We were downtown in Times Square; Sly was trying to catch the 9:00 tip. He finally beat for a wallet. We went into one restaurant in the Howard Johnson's Hotel to eat. We got into a big argument because he wanted me to wait until he finished eating to light my cigarette. I lit it anyway, he grabbed at my hand, I picked up the steak knife and stood up, and he slapped me and the next thing I know I was falling backwards. On top of that to pay for our food he hands the waitress the credit card he had just stolen, the credit card declined, the police came in asked him his name, he says something totally different than what's on the card. We both go to jail for criminal mischief. When we get to central booking we were processed and put into the bull pen, my stomach started to hurt really bad. One girl told me that I was in labor. Hell, I didn't know because the only other time I had been pregnant was at fourteen and I had miscarried then.

The pain was really getting unbearable. So finally they called me out and said they were taking me to the hospital in Queens. When I got there the nurse told them I was only six centimeters, so they had to take me back to central booking. I was hand cuffed the whole time. Well the bailiff said she didn't want to be responsible for me having the baby in the bull pen. Somehow they manage to get me on the roster for court. The district attorney tells the judge I'm a parole violator. The judge said he didn't care. He would not be responsible for me having that baby there. He released me for thirty days, after which time I was to turn myself in. Yeah, right!

I caught the train uptown wondering had they let that stupid motherfucker out too. When I got uptown. I saw two of my friends from Chicago standing in front of the Riverton. They told me they had some work and asked me if I wanted to go work it. I told them to let me bath and change clothes. We went up on Broadway and hit three banks. I ended up getting nine hundred dollars for my end. I was happy with that. We were on our way back uptown when my water broke. I was screaming and hollering because the pain was coming really, really bad. Once we made it to Harlem Hospital we had to go through the front lobby because the baby was coming fast. I was in so much pain. I thought I was going to die. They checked me, and then got me ready to go into the delivery room. The nurse looked at me like I wasn't shit. I guess she figured I smoked crack.

I had my son and he weighed six pounds, ten ounces. The doctor came in and talked to me after I came out of recovery he told me that they found large quantities of cocaine in my son's system, that they would have to keep him ten days for observation. Within those ten days I had to come to the hospital three times a day and feed him. Also I needed to give them an address so they could check out the house that I would be living in. The seriousness of what the doctor was saying didn't even register to me. I was just that far gone.

After I came out of recovery and was put in a room they let me go to the nursery to see my son and feed him. I named him after his father, Sonny Boy but we called him Lil Willie. My connect and a close friend of hers came up to bring me some clothes and to see the baby. I don't know to this day what made me leave that hospital. Yes, I do and for me to say different would be me being in denial, still after sixteen years. The craving for crack was so strong. It was stronger than my maternal instinct to stay in that hospital and see about my son.

Just by me knowing I had that nine hundred dollars in my pocket, I got nauseated and I felt like I had diarrhea. I needed a hit and I needed it right then. I got up, took me a shower. All the time thinking that I'm just going to go get me a hit and I'll be back. I left the hospital and about five hours later my connect came and found me she said "Bitch those people are looking for you at the hospital." I was so high, I never considered I had left my son, or that I had just had a baby and it was freezing out there. I was fucked up. The seriousness of what I had done still had not registered. The social worker called me in her office she asked me to give her an address that me and my son would be staying at, and reminded me about his feedings. The plan was to give them my connects address, and once we got out of the hospital we would catch a bus and go to Birmingham. I was so high I have them the wrong address and to top that off I missed a whole day of my son's feeding. The head nurse informed me that my son was going to foster care and if I wanted him back I had to go to court. They let me sit with him the night before they took him away.

I had promised myself that if I had ever had any children that I would always fight for them no matter what and never put a man before them. The fact that I had a child and didn't know where he was killing me softly. I didn't know what to do. I was strung out on the crack, literally just fucked up. I would stay up four and five days at a time. I couldn't sleep. I couldn't eat, wondering where the fuck my baby was.

Finally, one day I guess the staff got tired of seeing me because I went to the hospital everyday trying to find out where he was. They told me the foster agency was called Miracle Makers.

I called, they gave me my workers name and I made an appointment. She said I could come Thursday at twelve noon. I could see my son and meet the foster parents. James and I had mad amends with each other he was still hurt over the fact that my mama had left him for Doc. So on top of my shit I had to hear that all day. Thursday came around and I and James caught the train to Brooklyn. I was nervous as hell. The foster parents were already there. I met my social worker and she introduced me to the foster mom. She handed me my son, and at first he cried a little bit. I started humming "Thanks for My Child," That boy looked up at me and smiled, he was only three months but he knew who I was. Tears were streaming down my face. I just hugged him the whole time. I was there and talked to him. My worker set up times I could come see him. Every two weeks on Thursday. I thought somehow someway I needed to get myself together. I was so strung out on the crack I couldn't see one day for the next.

Sly was still around. Seems like after I had the baby he beat me more than ever. I hated Sonny Boy with every bone in my body. I felt like he could have kept those people from taking my son. The only excuse he could give me was. "I told you to go back to Birmingham but you didn't. So I don't want to hear that shit."

We were downtown working one day and Sly asked me a question. I guess I didn't answer quickly enough for him. We were standing in front of Bloomingdale's and he slapped me in front of all those people. I took off and started running down toward the subway; he caught me and was trying to throw me over onto the tracks. Some people saw him and grabbed him. They told me to go ahead get on the train. Several days later, I was uptown sitting in the car with a friend of mine named Ernie and something told me to look up, and when I did, I saw Sly running across Lenox Ave. He spotted me sitting in the car and headed that way. I locked my door and asked Earnie to do the same. He said he didn't want to get involved. I begged him "please lock the door." When Sly understood that I wasn't getting out he started kicking my window on the passenger side. The glass shattered all over my lap. He reached into the car and grabbed me by my hair and said "Bitch get out of the car!" When I opened the door to get out he kicked me in my face and I fell. It was about six people standing out there and nobody tried to stop him. He just kept stomping and dragging me. As I tried to get up he kicked me in my stomache and said "If your pregnant bitch I hope the baby dies!" I looked up and there was a police car coming down the street. I ran into the middle of the street and flagged the police down, a female officer got out. I was crying so hard I could barely tell her what happened. They arrested him and took me to the hospital. I was released the next morning.

With Sly out of the way I was able to go back around the hotel. I was pregnant again so I asked my connect for some work and she hooked me up. Amazingly Sonny Boy was still cool but he made it his business to say "I told you about them nothing ass niggas. I didn't want to hear that shit. He was like the rebound guy. Anytime something went wrong he was always there to pick me up.

I ended up getting arrested again around March of 1989. I went to Rikers Island. That was like a miniature Harlem. Drugs were everywhere. I always hung out with the girls from Brooklyn because I knew most of them from the street. After all my test had been done the doctor told me I really was pregnant and that I was having twins. I was put in the dorm where all the pregnant girls were. A few of my home girls were in there too. The way we fought in there it's a wonder I didn't deliver before time.

After I got convicted to another 1 ½ to 3, I got shipped back upstate. But this time I had to stay at Bedford because I was pregnant. That was the worst five months of my life. Everybody I tried to contact on the street suddenly disappeared. Because I had kept up with my visits at the agency, my worker made sure that the foster mom bought Willie to se me every two weeks. In New York State as long as the biological mother keeps in contact with their child they won't terminate your parental rights.

I got by on the food they served in the prison and one of the older drag broads was there who I called my aunt. She would always tell me to give her a list of the things I needed and she would get it for me every time she made store. I deeply appreciated that. There was a nursery at Bedford and if a person qualified they were able to keep their baby with them for a year. I filled out the application and everyone told me to be honest about my drug use and I did.

I went to have my babies January 8, 1990. I cried so hard because I could not believe that I had two babies at one time. My daughter came first weighing five pounds and ten ounces, my son weighed five pounds.

I named them after me and my mom. Patricia and Anthony. I didn't want them out of my sight. I use to prop both of them up on of my pillows so I could look at them. Sometimes I would fall asleep with them right there. Patricia looked like a little African and Anthony like a little old man. They were mine and we connected off the top. I had a c-section and was allowed to stay in the hospital five days. On the fourth day the officer came to tell me that my application had been denied. The prison said that needed to address my drug problem.

To this day I know that God has been my light and salvation. I was so hurt, and I cried until I made myself sick. Where were they going to go? I didn't have any family here. The family I had down south didn't give a fuck. I called my case worker and asked if they could get my babies. She told me yes but she didn't think they would be together. I told her that whatever she did, to please not separate them because they were all each other had, and they had to be together!

My worker found someone, and she told me that once she made all the arrangements I would be able to see the twins. The day I left that hospital. I thought I was going to die. My babies were still in that hospital and would be there until my worker picked them up. I stayed depressed almost three weeks. I wanted to die. I wanted to know what kind of God would let me go through this. Just go ahead and take my life because I wasn't living anyway.

On January 20, Patricia and Anthony's foster mother brought them to see me. You would have thought that I had won the lottery. I hugged them and cried until I couldn't see.

I didn't get out of prison again until 1991. Same shit different year, except for now the Riverton was closed. The new spot was the Ebony on 112th and 7th. I stayed in the halfway house a couple of days. Then I left. I had seen Sonny Boy up on Lenox. He gave me money then I went down on 112th. By this time word had spread that I was out. After I had been there a couple of hours later, June Bug came down. It was something about him this time around that I really wasn't feeling him. Then to top that he was fucking with a female that had AIDS. He knew she had Aids, but he didn't care. All he was concerned about was her getting money. He even had the audacity to say he wanted to see us in bed together. That nigga had straight bumped his head.

I woke up one morning and this nigga had a dirty white girl in the room. I got up open the door and kicked that bitch clean, through the door. This crack shit was getting out of hand.

There were a lot of Chicago boys around there at this time. I always went to work with one of them whose name was Chicago. He was really quiet, and everyday we would come from work he would go straight to his room. Chicago very attractive but I couldn't act like I liked him around June Bug because he wouldn't let me work with him.

I was still visiting my children every two weeks. There were times June Bug would tell me I couldn't go see my children. I would act like I was going to work and catch the train to Brooklyn and visit my kids, and tell him when I got back that I couldn't get any money. I was walking around and it felt like I was in a dream. June Bug was doing his thing. Sometimes he would leave and not come back for three or four days. I didn't give a fuck either because that was the only time I had some peace. He came one evening and told me that he wanted me to go to work with his new girl. I knew the days he was gone that, he was with her. We constantly fought because I wouldn't let him have sex with me. The next morning she and I went to work. I was very tired from staying up all night. We decided that we were going to go over to New Jersey I slept all the way over there. Then to top that off, they caught a lame and I slept through all of that. Needless to say, she couldn't wait to get back to tell June Bug. He jumped on me and then cut me in the back of my leg. Once he realized that he had cut me he started saying he was sorry and whole bunch of other weak shit. I had people actually coming up to me saying if I wanted them to do something to June Bug they would. He had been making a lot of enemies and they were running out of patience with him. that shit about him killing Bluebeard had played out, and he had crossed too many people. The next afternoon I saw June Bug and Chicago talking. Chicago was asking June Bug if I could go to work with him and Snoop the next day. We had been working together since Chicago had been in town. I remember him telling me one day "I'm not trying to get in your business little sister, but you should send some of your money home for a rainy day." I really appreciated the advice, but even if I did send money home there was no one there I could trust to send it to. Later on that day June Bug's girl had stung so her and June Bug was up in my room, and a few other friends, cocaine was everywhere. June Bug was sleep but he told me to keep an eye on her, that if she tried to leave wake him up. I sat up all night with them smoking cocaine, and then at one point I felt that I was having an out of body experience, because it seemed as if I was above them, watching the sad shape that my life was in. I thought "Is this really what my life has come to?" I had forgotten that I was supposed to be going to work with Chicago. So when he knocked on the door the next morning it was around 7:00 a.m. He asked me was I ready to go? I told him I was tired. He was like "come on it isn't going to take but a minute" So me, him, Snoop, and this girl name Pam went down town. That was the last day that I would see freedom for two years. I hadn't even been home a good two months and already I was on my way upstate.

When I got to Rikers Island I called the director of the agency I told him to go ahead and put my children up for adoption because I kept messing up their lives and that it wasn't fair to them to keep doing them like this. He told me that he wasn't going to do that because I was one of the mothers that really cared for my kids. He told me to call once I got myself together then we would set up a time for them to visit. There were times in my life that I thought I could go on. I was so goddamn tired of carrying this world on my shoulders. Nobody told me different. Today I understand that it had been written. This was my journey to travel.

While I was on Rikers I met this girl named Mona on visitation. She was a friend of my ex-girlfriend Precious. Precious was visiting her girl and asked if I would come on visitation and holla at her friend. I met her and we hit it off pretty well. She started looking out for me and making every visit even when Precious didn't come. One day I told her "listen I'm getting ready to go away for two years. I don't want to lie to you, so you can decide if you still want to holla or not." She was like "okay" is it something specific that you need me to do?" I told her yes "Act like you're my sister on my father's side and go get my children." and she did. She went through all the red tape with the case workers and lawyers. I was shipped to Bedford.

Mona would bring them there to see me, I only stayed at Bedford two weeks this time, and then I was shipped to Albion. They wouldn't let you do transfers anymore, the only way you left Albion were to go home or you got in some kind of trouble there. This time I stayed almost a year before I was shipped. While I was there I went to segregation for a sex offense, fighting, and being in an unauthorized area. Mona brought the kids to see me every month, plus she had a daughter too. I had started kicking with this soft-stud named Kelly. She was real popular around the camp and in love with me. I loved her as much as I knew how to that time.

I went to segregation a day before Mother's Day. Mona and the kids were coming to see me that Sunday. I told Kelley to call Mona and let her know that I was in lock up. Well from what I gathered on visitation the next day Kelley had gotten smart with Mona on the phone. The visit was horrible. Mona kept asking me was Kelly and I together, I asked her "why?" She said because of the way Kelley had talked to her on the phone. After a while Mona stopped coming to see me but she still wrote to me and sent packages. Then after a while I didn't hear from her at all. Then I got a letter notifying me that my children were back in foster care. That hurt me to my heart and clearly she knew it would. Because she knew how I felt about my children. Now I had to worry about who they were with, and were they being taken care of.

I talked to my caseworker and she assured me that they had very nice foster parents and that they were doing well. I got shipped to Camp Beacon a couple of months later around February of 1993. While I was at Albion I kept hearing about this female officer down in Beacon that liked tall dark skinned girls. Of course I was on it. Then to top it off they put me in the dorm where she was a regular officer 7-3 p.m. shift. I got a chance to meet her and to my delight she was, gay. I looked at her like she was a victim. I had to get mine and she would do just fine. I never considered that I could hurt people by my actions. I felt that everyone was out to get me so I had to get them first.

From the time I first got to that unit to the end she was on it. Then I would drop little lugs and let her know I was with it. Soon we stopped playing games and let each other know up front that we were attracted to each other. I because I liked what she would benefit me, money, clothes, calling checking on my kids. What ever I needed her to do she did. She had got to the point where she didn't even want me having a girlfriend on the camp. On days when there was no one in the unit she would come in my room after I got out of the shower and hit it.

Then the shit hit the fan. Anytime she mailed me stuff I told her to mail it from the city so if any thing ever went down they couldn't trace it back to her. I wasn't working in the kitchen any more. I was on a crew. There were nine crews on the camp that went out and did different public services like paint, build, clean the parks all kinds of stuff. Well, I was on crew 1. The officer on our crew was on vacation, and a female officer was filling in for him. We were out on a site building a house and my C.O. pulls up. It is her day off so she has her civilian clothes on. She said she had to use the restroom so the fill in officer told me to show her where it was. When we got upstairs she told me she had just finished sending my box off. On her way down the stairs she leaned over to kiss me, at the same time another inmate was coming up the stairs. We didn't think anything of it until a week later when administration called us in off of our site. When we were pulling in I saw my C.O. standing on the front of the unit. I told one of my friends to go over there and tell her that I would go down before I let her down.

There were two investigators in the room. They told me to have a seat. Once I sat down they started yelling at me, "Are you and that officer having a relationship?" I said "The only relationship me and that officer is having is an inmate officer relationship." I said "She's a good officer and she treats every one the same." When they saw that I wasn't going to bulge. They confiscated all my mail, package list, and phone records to see if we communicated that way. Not! They couldn't ask her were we having a relationship because then they would have been implying that she was gay. That's slander and she would have been able to sue them. The only thing they did was move her to transport.

As if I wasn't having enough problems her girl friend started harassing me on 11-7 passing by my cube saying little shit to me. One night she stopped I said "You must ain't doing what your supposed to be doing at the crib or your bitch wouldn't have to get it at the prison" My two friends was "Bitch no you didn't?" I said "I'm sick of that bitch fucking with me." And she's not going to write me up because she's going to have to explain why she keeps fucking with me! When I looked up she was in the officer station crying. So I guess the reality of what was going on really hit her. My C.O. had told me not to sweat it because they were on the verge of breaking up before I came along.

After a while the shit died down but it didn't stop anything. About a week later I got called to administration. The officer said I had an emergency and that I needed to call home. Now I'm freaking out because the only family I have in New York was my kids and this wasn't a 205 it was a 212 number. When I called the number a dude answered the phone. I told him someone called from this number wanted Toni to call. He said "Little sister it's me Chicago" I was like "Oh shit you scared me" He said that he was in town and he wanted to know how he could come visit me. I told him and he said that he'd be to see me on Saturday. I was really excited because I had always like Chicago, and he never treated me with nothing but respect. Also, when I first got this bid he looked out for me on Riker's. He also told me if I ever needed anything to write or call his mama in Alexander City, Alabama.

True to his word he started visiting me and he was straight looking out. Money, packages the whole nine. After awhile I asked him what were we doing? He said "Well take it as it comes." My C.O. didn't like the fact that a nigga was coming to visit. She felt like she could take care of me and I didn't need no one else. I tried explaining to her that Chicago was my friend but that was like talking to a wall. On top of all that I was fucking with this stud broad and she was giving me fever about the C.O. and, about Chicago. I was like damn chill! Plus I had just go my work release papers so she was tripping thinking she wouldn't hear from me after I left, but I promised her I would and that my word was bond.

The Friday of the week I was suppose to leave. I had to go to family court. I was frantic because I was going to miss this transfer but they assured me that once I got back I was still going to work release. My C.O. was my transfer officer she couldn't say too much because there was a male officer with her. Once I got to Rikers my court date was the following day. While I was down there Chicago came to see me plus I had a visit with my kids so those three days were straight.

The night I got back to the camp, I called Chicago to let him know that I'd be to work release on Friday, and also that in order for me to come out I had to have an address for verification. We used his address and the lady that owned the building act as if she was my grandmother. Friday came and I was transferred to the work release which is on 119th and Park Avenue. Chicago lived on 118th between 7th and Lenox. After everybody got finished being orientated they realized that I was the last one and they didn't have a bed for me. I told them I lived around the corner. They asked was there anyone around there that could verify that and I told them yes, my grandmother.

They called to verify and told me to be back tomorrow evening no later than 8:00 p.m. Chicago came and picked me up, he asked if I was hungry. I told him yes. So we walked up to the Chinese restaurant on 7th. It was a lovely night September 1993. Once we got back to his apartment we ate, talked. I called Birmingham to talk to my moms. I called Virginia to talk to my sister. I was so happy to be out. I didn't know what to do. But I did know this, those two ½ years gave me time to really look at my situation. I realized if I went back to June Bug I would continue to go down. I was determined not to do that because my children needed me, and I needed them, and I would do anything and anybody. I weighed my options and stayed with Chicago.

Part 3

Victory

THE NEXT DAY Chicago took me shopping, got me a pager, and personal hygiene items and an overnight bag. I was on five and two. Which meant that I was out five days and in two. My group was B group. We were to report in on Wednesday's and leave out on Friday morning. My requirements for work release were narcotic anonymous, parenting, urine drops, also to report to my parole officer at the center. Chicago wasn't a clingy type guy he felt if you were going to be with him then be, if not, then go. The first weekend I told him I was going to Brooklyn to hang out with my friends. Actually I was going to visit my C.O. We hung out, laid up did our thing, and I also found out she was a heroin user so that turned me off. She would call and ask me when she could see me and I just told her straight out "You lied to me. You told me that the only time you used was when you were younger." Now that I think of it, when she was at work, she would always, be sweating, and saying she was sleepy. Seems like every corner I turned there was a dead end. But I was determined not to go back to using.

In one of our conversations Chicago asked me what I wanted most in the world. I told him to get my kids out of foster care, and to visit my moms and my sister. I hadn't seen them in over eight years. Chicago told me he knew this lawyer and she only dealt in criminal cases, but by her being a personal friend she'd take the case, and her office was over in Brooklyn. She told Chicago that the retainer fee would be thousand dollars and five hundred every time she had to go to court. Chicago told her it was no problem. She set up an appointment for me to see her on Monday and for me to pay her, also to get familiar with the case. I met her and we hit it off pretty good. She told me she'd see me in court.

Chicago and I was getting along good too because he was a very good influence, and a good man to me. Which scared me a lot because nobody had ever treated this way before; deep down inside I felt that he wanted something too. I just couldn't figure it out yet.

Before I went in on Wednesday, Chicago told me he had bought me a plane ticket to fly to Virginia. That's where my sister was staying at, at that time. I flew over there that Friday. When I got there Trice and her boyfriend Von met me at the airport with her oldest son, Greg and her daughter, Diona. She was also pregnant. We cried like it was a funeral or something, acting like Cealy and Nettie from "The Color Purple."

My sister was my heart. I'm five years older so she was actually like my first child. When I use to run away I would always sneak back around my grandmother's house to give her money or clothes I bought for her.

We went skating that night then stayed up all night getting caught up on our lives. I left that Sunday but reassured her that we would come for Christmas. I cried all the way back to New York. I felt like I was missing something but I couldn't put my finger on it. Chicago met me at the airport. He let me know that the lawyer set up visits up for every Tuesday. I had that to look forward to, and I had a job working as a receptionist. My duties there were to type up reports, run errands, answer phones, numerous other small tasks.

Now that I had a job I only had to report to the center to see my parole officer and that was it until my parole hearing which would be February of 1994. It was already the end of October, 1993. I was working, visiting my kids, and making my court appearances at family court. In order for me to get them back I had to have a room specifically for my children, get burglary bars on the windows, maintain a job, and stay out of prison. In the meantime Chicago was going downtown every morning and once he got a sting he would call me and I would take my hour for lunch, go work the work he had, and then go back to work. I got off work every evening at 5:00 pm.

I met this girl at work release and she and I became really close, her name was Jeanette and I liked her style so we hung out a lot. I wasn't home but a month and already I had stacked my paper. I flew home to Birmingham for Thanksgiving, to see my mom. I realized today that back then no matter what I still had the hope that my mom would love me. I still looked at her and wanted her acceptance.

In 2004, I watch this movie called "Woman Thou Art Loosed" I remember Bishop T.D. Jakes saying "There's a little girl inside of you that needs to come out, that needs to live and be free." That line stood out so much for me because I was that little girl and all I ever wanted was to do was to be a little girl, and for my mama to step up one day, hug me, and tell me how much she loved me. She never did and I think that, that's the reason I hug and tell my children I love them constantly. My mama always had the tendency to forget anything that had to do with the past so often times when we were around each other I was amazed that she could act like nothing never happened and we were one big happy family. But I knew that one day I was going to get fed up with our facade and it was going to be ugly.

I stayed in Birmingham for four days at my mama's house; she was married again to this man named Floyd. For me I could never understand why this lady always had to have a nigga around her. Like she would die if she didn't have me. The sorry motherfucker didn't have a job and all he did was sit around the apartment and look ugly.

While I was in Birmingham, I went over to Collegeville, and as soon as I pulled up I saw a man leaning under the hood of the car. I knew it was my husband even before he stood up. He looked at me as if he had seen a ghost, blinked, looked again and knew it was reality. He walked over to me and said "I've dreamed of a hundred ways to kill you, but all I can think of now is how much I love you." And he hugged me and kept looking at me I guess to see if I was real. It's sad all the men that would have been good to me I ran as fast as I could.

My mind couldn't, wouldn't let me register that a person could love me for me. And if I start caring then it definitely had to be over because everybody I had tried to love crossed me. It's sad the coward, perverted ass man tuned my world upside down the day he touched me and took my innocence.

I believed that if I had let Chucky in my heart we would have been happy, but I couldn't and by his confessing his love to me scared me even more. He came over my mama's house for Thanksgiving. Then we visited his mom and sisters at their house. We ended up spending the night together and the next morning I left, going back to New York. I told him I'd see him again but I didn't know when, but I'd call. I walked away with a lot of feelings, and because I didn't know how to channel them. I always made bad choices.

My mom and my sister had made plans that we would meet at my sister's house in Virginia for Christmas. It would be our first time together in a while, and my mom and sister would see my children in person.

Once I got back to New York it just felt like I was drained so I had to re-energize. Chicago was being real supportive of me getting my kids back he even bought me a car so I could go back and forth to Brooklyn. I remember one Tuesday it was raining so hard but we still got in a cab and made it to my visit. When we got there the children were in the other room my worker told me she needed to speak to me a minute about something. Chicago said he'd go ahead and sit in there with the kids. As I'm standing there talking Mona comes out of nowhere and says to me "Toni I need to talk to you." I said, "Hold on don't you see me talking" The next thing I know this bitch has punched me in my face. I was too out done. I ran in the other room to tell Chicago. He and Mona got into a fight outside of the agency, it was so embarrassing. I just played it off and told my worker that my sister was angry because I hadn't spoke to her since I been out. She asked me why and I said, "Because she wanted my kids back."

Anyway what my worker was trying to tell me was that I could start getting my children for the weekend now. I was to pick all three of them up on Friday and bring them back Monday. On our way back to the city Chicago was going off talking about "I told you abut that punk ass shit." I was like "whatever" I really didn't want to hear that shit. The day before, we had already got into a beef about Paris the girl I use to mess with at the camp. He couldn't understand why I wanted to go see her and make sure she had the things that she needed.

I just knew how it felt to be left fucked up in a situation and not have anyone there for you. I kept my promise and went to see her like I promised her I would. Also she had been calling me and writing to me. This nigga had got to the point where he was opening my mail. I told him that to stop communicating with her wasn't an option the girl had looked out for me before he came along and it wasn't right that I just turn my back on her. That didn't last long, after I started visiting her, she wanted me to come every weekend. Which was impossible. I was on probation and had no business there in the first place. I didn't have to fight with Chicago anymore. She actually played herself. She called me one night and I wasn't home but Chicago accepted the call anyway. She asked him who he was and he told her. One thing leads to another then she tells him "I was with Toni while she was here." He said, "I'm with her now!" That's the part I caught as I was walking in the door. After that episode I didn't fuck with her no more. Christmas was approaching fast and we were going to Virginia, my mama, and James would meet us over there. I had sent for my cousin Rashaun to come to New York so that he could help me make my uncle Maurice comes home. My uncle Rome had died in 1989. He was the oldest after my mom and then Maurice. It seemed as if after Rome died; Maurice just started to go downhill I think it was because they were pretty close.

Every other week he was being hospitalized. Of course he was my family so I would go to the hospital to see him, and he was my favorite uncle. So I'd take him socks, underwear, whatever he needed. Maurice was what we called a vet in the con-game, everyone wanted to work with him because he was one of the best.

He got his disability check at the first of the month, and his pain medication was deluded so every dope fiend in Harlem wanted to be his friend. But soon as the money ran out, someone was calling me, telling me to come get Maurice. When Maurice got high he would sit in one place for hours, even after the dope and money had ran out. I was tired of getting up out of my bed in the middle of the night.

Everyone planned to meet at my sister's house for Christmas. Me, Chicago, Maurice, Rashuan, and my children. Rashaun and Maurice were going to ride back to Birmingham with my mama and James, after the holidays.

December 20, I was supposed to be in court for a review. I had already gotten permission from the agency to keep my kids throughout the Christmas holidays. When I got to court the judge said that my children were being released to me for a 90 day trial basis. Oh, my god I couldn't believe it. I had done it; my children were finally coming home. I hugged everyone in that courtroom. My case worker told me to pick the children up the following day at the agency and she wished me good luck. I was so full of joy, and I looked at Chicago and hugged him and thanked him, ad thanked God. I didn't know that on down the line that I would hear how appreciative I should be for him getting my children out of foster care.

The day came for me to pick up my children. Patricia was standing by the door with her Barney doll, Anthony was sitting in a chair. When he seen me he took off running towards me. Patricia kept asking me "are we going to my Barney bed?" I told her "Yeah!" Willie was standing over on the other side of the room and I was telling him that it was time to go. His foster mother started crying. Willie was crying. He didn't want to go and I was torn because that was my son and the judge gave them back to me but on the other hand, Willie had been with this lady four years. Although, I was his mother. I had no right to make him hurt like that. I would regret my decision years later. I let him stay until we could agree on what we were going to do.

I told the agency and my worker that I'd see them after the Christmas holidays and we could work something out then. I was so afraid to take my children home. I was afraid that I'd be like my mama, or that I couldn't care for them properly. I didn't know the first thing about children.

On the 23rd I got a call from the attorney for the agency saying if I didn't bring the children I was going to be charged with kidnaping. Oh, my God. Chicago was like "calm down and let me call our lawyer." She told me not to panic, that she would handle if from there. And she did.

We drove to Virginia that day. We had most of their toys and gifts in the trunk. It seems like it took forever to get there. We finally made it. My sister had moved to a townhouse. A much bigger place than the one she had before. About an hour later my mama and James showed up. Everybody hugged and kissed my kids because nobody had ever seen them before. We danced, laughed we had a blast that first night. Christmas Eve my mama and Trice cooked. Greg, Diona, Patricia and Anthony were still trying to figure each other out. My mama asked about Willie, and I told her what happened. During the middle of the day I was standing by the fireplace, my sister was like "You're pregnant." I laughed it off because if I was, and I calculated right. Then it was a problem because when I went to Birmingham for Thanksgiving I was on my cycle, well going off of my cycle and I and Chucky had been intimate. I just wasn't going to think about it then. Because if my dates were correct then it was a problem.

Above all we had a good Christmas except for the time when my mom, James and Maurice were high and nodding all over each other. My sister and I were so embarrassed that Chicago and Von had to see that. We were use to it by now.

The day after Christmas, Chicago, the twins and I started back towards New York. I felt so tired. Anthony and Patricia were in the back seat looking out the window. They were tickled to death about all the sights that they were seeing. Especially when we were going across the Cheasepe Bridge. It was suppose to be the longest bridge in the United States. I got really sick after we came off of the bridge. My stomache was cramping up and everything. Chicago pulled over to a gas station so I could get some pepto bismal. I thought it was something I ate, but now that I look back I know it was the heroin I had been sniffing. I had caught a habit in just that short time. The one thing that I promised myself I'd never do, I had been doing, and on top of that I had to go to the center on Monday and give them urine. The only thing I could think about is, if I came back with dirty urine Chicago wasn't going to understand it.

All weekend I drove myself crazy about it. Finally Monday came but I didn't know the results until Wednesday. You know its funny how our minds work to justify our behavior. I actually felt that I wasn't doing anything wrong, shit! I just wanted to be high for the holidays. I was slowly headed for a self destruction.

To keep my mind off of Wednesday, Patricia and I hung out on 125th street shopping and taking pictures. Anthony hung out with Chicago getting his hair cut, men stuff. On Sunday, January 8, 1994 we gave Anthony and Patricia a birthday party at the McDonald's on Columbus Avenue. I even had Willie for the weekend too. He always did well as long as he didn't have to spend the night. Although, that hurt me I invited a few of our friend's kids and it turned out pretty good. I had moments that I would just look at my children and think to myself that these are really mine, and I am responsible for them. Monday rolled around, and I had to take Willie back to the agency. I spoke to my worker and I told her that I'd be taking the twins back to Birmingham with me and if they needed me for anything concerning Willie to call me and I'd come back. She explained to me about an open adoption. She said that with an open adoption there could be a clause in there that said that the adoptive parent agrees to sibling visits. I told her that's the only way I would sign because I wanted my children to know each other.

I had made it up in mind that Willie was more of his foster mother's than mine. Even though I gave birth to him. I had no right to mess his life up forcing myself on him. It hurt like hell that he preferred this lady over me but I had to let him go. We would be leaving sometime in March but up until then we would still visit Willie. I told his foster mother that we would be calling and writing to him also. She agreed. I went in to report on Wednesday you would have thought I was walking into a gas chamber. My urine was clean. It was days like this that I knew that when I got tired of walking God was carrying me. I just didn't know how to receive it. Back then I said it was luck. I actually thought I was getting over only time would tell.

Chicago didn't know that I was planning on going back to Birmingham, I would tell him eventually. Everything just felt like it was closing in on me. My mama said she had cancer, Chucky kept calling, I found out I was pregnant, and the only girl that I let myself love was on the scene. I found out later that my mama was a hypochondriac but because I had a chance to be around her, I looked over that. The little girl in me wanted her love so badly, that I just kept searching for the connection. Why couldn't I see that it wasn't going to happen?

The girl that I was in love with name was Lisa Felder. Everyone called her Spoonie. We met in Bedford on my second bid. She made it plain to me that she was in love with her wife Diane and wasn't looking for a commitment. I wasn't trying to hear that shit so I pursued her, until she gave in. Lisa was really cool and laid back so that's what I think attracted me to her, plus the way she carried herself. We instantly became an item. No sooner than we got comfortable. Lisa got shipped to Albion. I was sick. I mean physically ill. I couldn't eat, I couldn't sleep. About two weeks later they told me to "pack it up." I was being transferred also to Albion. Lisa and I wrote each other faithfully, so I knew that she'd be happy that I was coming there.

We got to Albion late that evening after we were orientated the officer assigned us to a block. I was assigned to F building. Lisa was across from me in E. As we were walking to our block I could hear Lisa calling me "Yo Tonithia!" After the initial shock wore off we had our little routine.

Because we didn't live together we would meet on the yard or in the gym. Then if we had a cool officer we would sneak into each other's dorm and do our thing. I remember one evening after coming from the gym. This girl Sharon and I got into it in the bathroom. She was a stud. She told me to kiss her ass and I lit her ass up too! When I looked up Lisa was busting through the door and she tagged her ass too. All of us got fourteen days segregation time. When we came out of seg I got moved up the hill. So that meant I could only see Lisa at chow and in the evenings.

I noticed that she had been acting shady with me and talking shit. She'd say shit like "Get away from me." One day she just straight came out and said that she didn't want to see me anymore. Oh, my God. I couldn't foresee that! It wasn't even conceivable. I told the officer that I was going to kill myself. I can't even begin to describe how I was feeling. With a guy it didn't matter one way or another if we were together. But with a female it felt so much different. I wasn't gay or anything. I just like girls.

They put me in a padded room then the next day they moved me back to F block. It had got to me that Lisa was hollering at this other girl. But, the devil was a lie. It wasn't going down like that. So on my way from dinner I asked her to come outside, she said she wasn't coming she must have seen that look in my eyes. I asked her again "please come outside" And she did. I said "Tell me in my face you don't want to be with me, and she did." And I ate her ass up! All I did to get up in them damn mountains to be with her ass, then she gone trip. I don't think so. We both went to seg. The time we were in seg we sent each other letters apologizing a whole bunch of shit.

About a week after that I had to be transferred down state to go to family court plus I got a chance to see my children because Albion was so far upstate they never got a chance to visit so I wrote to them every week.

When I got back to Albion, Lisa had maxed out. I didn't see her again until I got arrested again in 1991. When I got to the Island word got around in population that I was back. Well, Lisa made it her business to come down there to bring personal items, food and a whole bunch of other stuff. When she gave me the bag she said, "I messing with somebody so please don't start no shit" I said "as long as you don't bother me I won't bother you. After they put us in a dorm, everybody was coming down to see if I needed anything. I told them I was straight. Well the next day I was out on the yard. Lisa came to me and said she wanted me back. I asked her really nice "if you're not going to do the right thing leave me alone" She said she was so we sat at rec and caught up, talked the whole time. I told her that I had to go to court tomorrow so I'd see her when I got back. I got back from court around two. Rec was still going on. I went outside. Once I got out there I immediately looked for Lisa. She was standing over by the bleachers talking to Tawana her suppose to be girlfriend. I headed in that direction. I said, "Lisa come her.!" That bitch turned around and said, "Can't you see I'm talking to my girl!" I don't do rejection well at all. I tore a new hole in her ass. The rec officer was holding say "Alabama that's enough!" I was trying to get at Twana too. The officer took me to lock up for a couple of hours. While I was in there I had a chance to think about the situation. I fell right into that bullshit. My attitude from here on out was "Fuck Lisa".

I got moved over to the old building. Lisa's girl was in the new building. Lisa and I would see each other at mealtime. She kept trying to get me to talk to her. I was giving that bitch pure fever. One day she stopped me in the hallway and was like you don't have to talk to me just let me be with you. I said alright cool but when you get on the other side act like you don't know me. That was easier said than done on her part because the whole time she was with her girl she was trying to see what I was doing.

Finally, her girl left to go to Bedford. Now she wanted to be serious but I was going to get that bitch back for every hurt and pain she ever caused me. We got back together, and we were in the same dorm, we both had jobs. But I was plotting hard. I was a suicide aid so I worked receiving making sure nobody was hanging themselves up, checking the new arrivals every thirty minutes. Most of them were kicking heroine, or coming off some type of drug.

Lisa would come pick me up everyday at 12:00 so we could go to lunch and then she'd walk me back. One day I got to work and during 11-7 shift they had brought in this really cute girl. Everyone called her

Dee. In Riker's, a person could wear their own clothes, so every day I was rocking something fly. Dee started flirting with me, I started flirting back. This went on for about two weeks, and then one day she just said wear a dress with no panties on and I did. Lisa came to get me. At 12 and I hadn't come out yet. So when I finally came out she was like "what the fuck took you so long!" It was my time to shine. I said "I was doing me!" She jumped like I had stabbed her when she looked up she had tears in her eyes and she said, "You told me that you forgave me, you promised me that we were through this!" Instead of feeling good about what I did I felt like shit. It took a whole week for Lisa to talk to me again and when she did it was like we started all over again. We were always together you didn't see one without the other.

We never or I never brought up the subject of her wife, maybe because I was still in denial. Shit. Her and this girl had been together for about six years. They had a history, how could I compete with that? I couldn't. I settled for what I could get right then and there. Lisa got shipped a couple of months later. We wrote to each other all the time. Thirty days after she was shipped so was I. But the day I got to Bedford was the day she went to Groveland. Basically we kept missing each other, but we kept in touch.

I'd been out since September of1992, and I'd been really busy. I didn't have time to think of Lisa, but it dawned on me that January of1994 was her release date. I went to the address she gave me and her son answered the door. He told me his mom wasn't there. I asked if he would giver her pager number, and phone number. Two nights later I got the call, she told me she was 113th between 7th and 8th. When I got down there I saw a bunch of niggas standing on the corner. Lisa stepped out but if I didn't know she was a girl I would have sworn that she was a boy. She got in the car, we hugged. Then we told each other how good the other looked, catching up. She told me she was still with Diane, and she said that it didn't mean anything. In my mind I thought, it means a lot to me. If she had of told me she was by herself. I would have got my children and left Chicago right then. But she wasn't.

We hung out that whole week, me her and the kids. She kept trying to get me to go to a hotel with her. I knew if I did. I would have never left New York and would have accepted the situation like it was. Chicago was still trying to get me to stay. I wasn't in love enough with him to stay. Besides my mama had cancer she needed me. Didn't she?

I finally told Lisa I was leaving. My parole was being transferred to Birmingham. I found out Anthony and Patricia's father, Sly, was out and was living six blocks from us. I definitely had to go. He got to see them, and take them shopping once before we left. I gave him my mom's phone number and told him if he wanted to talk to his kids he could call them. He never did.

The night before I left, Lisa and I rode around for a long time; she cried and asked me not to go. I cried too, but I told her I had to. I and the twins were supposed to catch a flight out of Newark airport the next day. My car ran hot and I accused Chicago of sabotaging the car because he didn't want me to leave. After we made it to the airport. I told Chicago I'd call once I got to Birmingham. We missed our flight so we had to sit in the airport another two hours. Once we arrived in Atlanta I got lost trying to get to the main terminal. I was pregnant, with two kids, and I had eight thousand dollars in my luggage in my luggage. I really needed to get to the baggage claim.

My mama and her husband were supposed to pick us up. I didn't see them anywhere so I had to find a phone booth to see if they had left Birmingham yet. Then all of a sudden I hear someone calling my name. It was my mama. I hadn't been so happy to see anyone as bad as I was to see her then. I was tired emotionally and physically, and my feet hurt. It was such a joy to finally get in the car and sit down. This would be the first time me and my mama stayed in the same house since I'd been grown. I was anxious to see how this was going to turn out.

I called Chicago to let him know I had made it. I had decided I'd call Chucky the next day because I was too tired to call right then. My mom had a job working at a nursing home and she had to be at work the next day. We all laid it down for the night. The twins were only four so I wasn't worrying about putting them in day care at that time. The next day I thought I was a celebrity the people were stopping at my mama's house. I found out to that my mom baby sister and one of her younger brothers was smoking crack. I should have packed my shit and left then, should have been scared but I wasn't.

Big, bad ass, Toni always had to prove something. My husband had started coming around more often and we would kick it or just chill. I had taken my children to see my grandma, she was so tickled that I had twins she said, "Hot damn that girl had two babies for real" W.C. was still staying with her too. I guess he was trying to stay out of my way whenever I came over. My uncle Maurice was home, he was staying in the apartment with us. My mama was told me about a broad, she said she sold dope and she was using my uncle as a flunky.

I finally met her one day coming out of Maggie's store. Maggie had been there since I was a little girl. Ole girl was cool, she had two daughters in high school, plus a son in elementary. She was trying to make ends meet like everyone else. My uncle was a grown ass man and if he wanted to be a flunky that was on him.

One day while I was cooking I kept noticing Chucky kept running in and out of the back door. I asked him where he was going. He told me to get something for Maurice. I asked him what? He said "crack" and I went off. I told him "You know how I feel about that shit so why would you go around there and get it for him?" Come to find out he had been smoking it too. When he left that day I told him "if you're smoking that shit you need to stay away from me. I was trying so hard."

After he had been gone a couple of hours I got worried. The phone rang; it was him saying that he was in the city jail for a DUI.

All it took was for one little thing to stress me out then I'd have a reason to smoke again. I was upstairs; my Auntie had been in there trying to get me to give her some money. As soon as I put the phone down I looked at her and said "go get me one" She was like "are you sure?" I said "Yes" and it got crunk up. I understand now that the reason I didn't smoke while I was with Chicago, is because he kept me away from all that, and he kept me busy. Deep down inside I really did want to get high. My aunt came back with the crack; I smoked that and kept sending her back for more. After I had calmed down and realized what I had done I cried and I cried.

I was once told that each time you go back and do crack your addiction gets worse. Whoever said it never lied. My husband got out of jail. I had forgotten how weak of a nigga he was anyway. I had sold most of my jewelry, and all this Negro did was sit around me and wait for me to give him some dope. My mama couldn't stand him, she had moved to West End in one house with Floyd. She and I constantly got into it because I discovered she took the money I gave her to pay rent with she spent, she got an attitude and told me I should have went and paid it myself. My uncle's wife and kids stayed next door to us.

I would send Anthony and Patricia over there for her to watch them sometimes when I got too high. I was calling Chicago to send me money, thinking of a new lie each time. One night I smoked up all my money and I was trying to figure out what my life had turned in to. I was very confused and didn't know where to turn to. I called Chicago again asked him if I could come back to New York. He told me that he was involved with someone else and he didn't think that it was a good time for me to come. I begged him. Because I knew if I stayed in Birmingham I was again headed for self-destruction. He still said no!

By this time I and Ole girl had become really cool. She would front me dope because she knew I would pay her off the top. Her sister and I became tight also. Sis would go out with me and watch my back while I was hustling. All the dope kids in the bottom knew that I did my thing. They would tell me that morning before I went out what they wanted me to get for them, outfits, all kinds of name brands. I had one rule; they had to pay me in money not dope. Some of them wouldn't sell to me because I was pregnant.

Especially, this one dude. He said I was too pretty, and on top of that I was pregnant. So he made it clear to me not to ask him to sell to me. My parole had been transferred to Birmingham, I had to go in every month to report and give urine because I had such a bad drug history. I reported to my parole officer between the first and fifth of every month.

It was time for my may visit. When I went in to see my parole officer, he told me not to bother sitting down. I had dirty urine and he wanted me to go to treatment as soon as I left his office. I made up some shit about I had to check on my children. He politely told me you have one or two options, you can leave here and go to the rehab or go to jail.

Needless to say once I got back in the car, I told my mama to go over to Ole girl so that I could cope some dope. My life had become so unmanageable, that I was using dope while I was pregnant, again. And this man was threatening to send me to jail. I just didn't give a fuck. I thought that if I went to jail, my mom would take care of my kids. I was traveling the same road that my mom had traveled, only faster. If I didn't detour sooner or later I was going to crash and burn.

The next morning Sis and I decided that we were going to go to work. We stopped by Ole girl's on our way. As we walked in the front room I saw a girl sitting on the sofa. I asked her, her name, she told me, Vee. I asked her to give me a Newport because I had left mine in the care, she told me no. I reached down in her purse and got it myself. I told her "my name is Toni" "I'm on my way to work now." "I'll be home around three p.m". "I live across the street from Norwood School in the brick apartments." "If you are interested be there at six o'clock." On my way out the door I heard Ole girl tell Vee "That bitch ain't no joke. Bitch don't go up in that house because you ain't gonna come out" I laughed all the way to the car. I had stopped Chucky from coming to my house and nobody lived there now but my children and me.

Maurice had left to go back on the road, and my other uncle stayed there sometimes. Vee showed up that evening. We kicked it, got high, and did our thing. And, Ole girl was right she didn't come back out of the house. Maya and I became a couple. It happened just like that. I realize now that our relationship was based on the dope more than anything. If we weren't getting high we were having sex. After a while it was just normal for us to be together.

One night me, my mama, and Ole girl were sitting in the front room, my uncle came through the back door and told me that Vee was down in the bottom dancing on the table. I walked down there with a two by four because I was going to beat her ass. When I got down there I knocked on the door and asked was Vee in there. I could hear her saying "don't open the door. That bitch is crazy." I told her, "bitch you got to come out of there, and when you do I'm going to fuck your ass up." When she did decide to come back around to my house. I told her to get out she was like, "I aint going no where. I said, "Oh, bitch you're going to get up out of here." She finally left.

After a couple of weeks I started kicking it was the dope kid name Sean. Sean wasn't one of the balling type dope boys he sold enough to stay above water, but his brother was balling. For some reason I always seem to attract the kind of niggas that were really needy. Sean smoked a lot of weed, and loved to hang down in the bottom or up the hill at the jook joint. Everybody hung out at the jook joint on Friday and Saturday nights.

Ole girl told me I was a fool for fucking with him because he was sorry. Every time I went out to work I would get him all the new shit that came out, plus put like five hundred to a thousand dollars in his pocket. Sad part about he never did anything with the money but blow it. I was always snapping on Sean because he thought that because I liked him he could handle me any kind of way. He was still tipping with his ex-girlfriend. So where ever I saw them at that's where I clowned at. All the dope boy's were like "damn dawg I wish I had a girl like that, "Shit, Toni I'll be your man.

Sean didn't know I got high because I always put up a good front. Soon as that nigga left out the house I was puffing. Then the day came where I just didn't give a fuck. Shit, "I bought my own dope, that nigga couldn't tell me what to do. It happened one day, I was in the front room getting high and he walked in the door. He was like "Ah man. You just like the rest of them." He said with a defeated look in his eyes "it's going to be me or the dope." I said "I'll holla."

I could tell he was hurt. I just didn't give a fuck. Things were quickly spiraling out of control. Chicago popped up in Birmingham and said he just came to see me and how I was doing. I was scared to death. Sean was down in the bottom and Chicago was sitting in the front room. Chicago kept trying to get me to go upstairs with him, and then Sean walked in the back door. I introduced them. Chicago waited till Sean left out to ask me if that was my boyfriend. I told him I needed some money. I didn't want to hear all of that other shit. He said he didn't have any cash on him, and that he had to go to the ATM. We went to the ATM; he gave me two hundred dollars. I was trying to figure out how I could get this nigga to leave. All I wanted was to get me some dope. I had really lost my goddamn mind.

We were driving past the gas station on Eighth Avenue. I told him to stop because I needed to get me some cigarettes. I really went in there to get a new stem to smoke my dope in. When we got back to my house I jumped out the car and was like "okay, bye" No hug, no kiss, and no nothing. All I was concerned about was getting some dope. My addiction had got really bad. Ole girl tried to get me to come out to her house in Centerpoint. She didn't want to sell me no dope, but she knew if she didn't I'd buy it somewhere else.

Sean had stopped speaking to me. I was selling the lady across the street my food stamps. My whole reason for breathing was for dope. I was seven months pregnant, and also had the twins with me. My dumb ass didn't think that I was neglecting them. I felt like as long as I fed them, bathe them and made sure they were clean I was a good mother. I and my moms weren't speaking. I came home from work one day all my shit was sitting outside. I had nowhere to go so we stayed in a hotel.

The weekend of the foot wash Sis and Ole girl asked me to go with them I declined. I just didn't see myself going that long without crack. That weekend while they were gone. I got someone to watch the kids for me while I and a friend of mine went to work. I ended up taking a wallet; we were on our way to the mall so I could use the credit cards. Come to find out the credit card belonged to the wife of their head of security. I was arrested for theft of property and once I got to county jail. I had three more warrants from AmSouth, Colonial, and SouthTrust banks. Because in my haste to get money, I was using other peoples checks and writing them to myself, my real name and using my real identification. My bond was fifty thousand dollars, plus I had a fugitive warrant from New York. I was finished or so I thought. Once again God would carry me through something I had gotten myself into.

I got upstairs; I found out that Vee was up here too. They had her on a charge and were trying to get her to tell on me for something they thought I did, but she held it down. When I got arrested my mom had went over to Centerpoint and got Anthony and Patricia. The only reason she did that was to get the food stamps and check. I finally went to court; while I was there my mom came and brought the twins. When Anthony seen me he snatched away from my mom and came into the area where inmates have to sit in court. And he hugged me so tight. The judge asked who child was it. I said "mine" He asked how many months was I. My attorney told the judge, that at my request I was ready to be sentenced so I could make it to Tutwiler before I had my baby. The judge said no, that I wasn't going to Tutwiler. I was going to treatment. He then instructed the probation officer to call New York and get the warrant off me, or he'd lift it himself. I was sentenced to fifteen years suspended for one year. Meaning that I was not to get into any trouble for a year. If I did I would have to serve the fifteen years.

My mom left with the kids and I told her I'd call as soon as I got where I was going. The judge told the bailiff to take the handcuffs off of me, and let me go in the back with my kids. I was assigned a Task officer; she was sort of like a parole officer. I would have to call a number everyday to see what my color was, which was gold. If gold come up then I had to go in the next day report to Task and pee. The treatment center I was assigned to was for females that were pregnant or had kids under the age of five. The house was located on the southside and when you stepped in there the place surrounds you with a sense of peace. My counselors were real straight forward, and they kept it real with me at all times. My Medicaid paid for the treatment.

Really all I had to do was follow the rules. They were mainly, no drugs, three meetings a week, make out pre-natal appointments and go to class Monday through Friday. Chicago sent me money every week, and movies that I could watch. He was really caring and generous to me during my pregnancy even though he was with someone else. He said it was hard for him to picture me on drugs while I was pregnant for him.

Then that Sunday mama brought my children over with their clothes and everything. I went over to the foodstamps office and let them know that my mom was no longer taking care of my children. She stopped speaking to me behind that. Why get my food stamps if my kids were not with her, why? But my kids and I were fine. I wasn't getting high. I was going to my appointments. I had three weeks before I delivered.

That following Saturday, one of the counselors that worked with us on the weekend took us out to Avondale Park, rumor was that one of the girls was smoking crack in the house. I told the counselor that I was leaving. I told her Judge Johnson sent me to get help. Bottom line I was scared that if I did see, smell it, or whatever I'd end up using again. I left and went over to Ole girl's house. My kids and I stayed there with her and her family. On August 22, 1994. I gave birth to Hassan. He was the most beautiful baby I had ever seen. I called Big Mama to let her know, and she in turn called Chicago. To University Hospital.

I kept dosing on and off. When I woke up again I was in the recovery room, then a private room. Sean was sitting over in the chair knocked out. I rung the nurse and asked if she could bring Hassan to me, she told me "yes, in a half hour." The phone rang I picked it up and it was Chicago. He asked how I was doing. Then he asked how he got to the hospital. I asked where he was. He told me airport highway. I gave him directions, hung up the phone, woke Sean up and told him he had to leave because Chicago was on his way. We got into a little verbal altercation. Bottom line was he had to get the fuck up out of there. I wasn't that big of a fool, Shit! I had just had the "Heir!" Sean left smoking hot, he got over it. No sooner than Sean left, Chicago came through the door. He had balloons, a big ass black leather bag, he hugged me and asked me how I was doing, and he asked where the baby was. I don't know what it was about Chicago, he was the perfect guy but I could never let myself go deep. Don't get me wrong, I loved him because he was a good dude to me and my kids. But it wasn't none of that get struck by lightning love. To be totally honest as I look back. I believed that I felt indebted to him, obligated even. But couldn't be around him too long because he irked the shit out of me, and he made me remember what I tried to forget about sex. A lot of times it made me really uncomfortable because as long as we had sex he was fine.

We walked down to the nursery, and when got in there I noticed this beige colored card taped to Hassan's crib. I asked the nurse "what was that for?" She told me that if a baby is born with anything in their system that hospital uses color coded cards so they could know exactly it was that they found. I asked, what did the beige mean? Because Chicago was on the side of me like he was getting ready to explode. She told me it was some kind of ingredient found in pills. She asked me what I had taken. I told her a codeine pill for pain before I came to the hospital.

Chicago sat up in that room and held Hassan until he couldn't hold him any more. He called Big Mama and let her know that we'd be down tomorrow after I got released from the hospital. Ole girl them came up that night, and my cousins, everybody except my mom. This lady was holding a grudge with me about some goddamn food stamps. What had I ever done to her?

I got out of the hospital the next day. Chicago took me and the baby to Kmart and bought everything he thought Akeem needed and didn't need. We went downtown to pay my lawyer for one case I had so he could go to court and let Judge Johnson know that I was doing okay. Then we went over to the Daycare Center where my grandmama worked, she said how pretty the baby was then she wore my ass out, "You out there in this weather with dis baby. Yo ass gone have a set back. When we got in the he car I asked Chicago where we were going. He said he was trying to beat the traffic on 280. Well, I wanted to get my hair done so I told him to drop me off at the beauty shop and go on with Hassan to Alexander City. After I finished getting my hair done, I called Ole girl and asked her to send somebody to pick me up. Said she'd send somebody but that I was a damn fool because I should have went with Chicago and the baby. After a while I started feeling empty, so I called Chicago at his mom's house and I was like "Bring me my baby." He said, "No!" Because he had just got there. I said "let me speak to your mama! He said "don't involve her" I said bring me my baby then. He didn't want me to speak to his mama because he knew that Big Mama would tell him to bring my baby back. So he said he'd bring the baby back tonight under one condition and I asked what is that? He said if I'd spend the night in the hotel with him. I hated, but I told him "yeah"

We were supposed to meet at the Civic Center Inn. He'd call me once he got there. I often wonder if I had of went with him then what would my life had of been like? I guess I won't know because I was told that nothing happens in God's world by mistake and that I'm doing exactly what I was put here for. Chicago brought me the baby and I spent the night with him just holding me with the baby in front of me. I felt really bad that I couldn't return that deep love that he had for me. The sad truth was I wasn't finished getting high so any thought of love or being sober was gone.

When we woke up the next morning he dropped up off at Ole girls. He told me if I found a place he would send me the money to get it, all could think of was if he send me the money how much dope I was going to buy.

Here I was with a week old baby, and two four year olds, and I didn't have a clue about tomorrow. Wouldn't it have just been simpler for me to surrender and let Chicago take care of me? Then I would have to give up the dope.

I ended up staying out at Ole girl's house. I would pay her daughter to watch my kids while I went out to work. Ole girl told me if she found out I was getting high I would have to leave her house. Even though she sold dope in the bottom, she didn't allow it to be sold out of her house in Centerpoint. When she found out I was using she told me to get my things and leave.

I checked into a hotel in North Birmingham, me and my three children. I called one of my childhood friends to let him know to pick me up the next morning so he could take me to work. After we came back from the mall, I stopped in Norwood to pick my kids up, but ended up chilling, getting high and by it being Friday night music was playing and everybody was having a good time. My dumb ass was in there doing the Tootsie Roll like I hadn't just had a baby a week ago. I woke up the next morning and could hardly walk so I sent for someone to come take me to Caraway Hospital. I left word for Ole girl to please get my children from the jook joint.

I ended up getting admitted to the hospital because my liver had swollen. I felt as if I had come to the end of my rope. My little cousin and her boyfriend had come up to see me and a few other people. I needed to get away for a while so I called Chicago, he agreed to send me a plane ticket, and after I was discharged I took Hassan to Alexander City. Ole girl agreed to keep Anthony and Patricia.

I got on a plane going to New York, September 7, 1994. I really wanted to clear my head and thought that this would be the best thing for me. Chicago picked me up from the airport; on the way to Harlem he told me he had a female living with him. I asked him "What does that have to do with me. I came to get some money." The first night I stayed there I already knew what he wanted to happen. Chicago enjoyed watching me and another female have sex. He said that it turned him on because I was so aggressive and took charge in that situation. The fact was that I felt very comfortable with females, and contact with them didn't bother me the way it did with a man.

I was so insecure and my self-esteem was so low that I actually thought I had to put myself through this degradation for him to except me, or to prove that I was down with him. Sometimes it felt I was in a dream or that I was outside of my body looking in. I felt nothing. All three of us slept together that night. She and I ended up having sex with each other while he watched. I always felt very uncomfortable that he had this fixation with seeing me with women in bed, but he talked about gay women like they weren't shit.

Chicago claimed he detested anybody doing drugs around him that's why he was so embarrassed that I found out Stephanie was smoking. That gave me the excuse I needed to go out and do the same. I went out that night and He kept calling my pager, I wouldn't answer. I finally came in about six am. He grabbed me like he was going to hit me, and I told him if you hit me I'm going to throw that bitch out of the window.

Once again he put me on a flight back to Birmingham. Chicago gave me money to look for an apartment. I got a weekly hotel and got high with the rest. I didn't know what was going on in the world, or what was it I was suppose to be doing. There were days I looked at my kids and hated what I had become a, crack head. I even went and got Hassan instead of leaving him down in Alexander City with his grandparents, in a caring environment. I thought about my family and it was sad I had no one to turn to. I was just tired. I was staying downtown in an efficiency hotel, the only food I had in the room was a box of Kix cereal, wic cheese, and a gallon of milk. All my clothes were dirty and I had no idea on how I would pay the rent from one day to the next. I had gone to court earlier that day and the judge told me that if he had someone take a newborn baby he would have locked my ass up then.

To this day I don't know who called Chicago and told him I was in that hotel, but he called and asked where I was. I told him. When he got to the room he just looked at me and the children. He hugged me and told me that in the morning we would get all the clothes washed, pay the room up for a week take Hassan to Big Mama, take the twins to Ole girl, and take me to get some help.

He went and got us some food and Hassan some milk; he wasn't even two months old yet. Chicago didn't judge me. I bathed the children, and he ran my bath water. I bathed and he held me all night telling me I would be okay. I'm glad he was confident about that cause I sure as hell wasn't. We got up the next morning and got ready to go, and I had all intentions of going. That deceitfulness set in and I told Chicago "You take the baby; I'll wait till you get back." I asked him if he would leave me some money he said "No!" When I thought he had pulled off, I left the twins upstairs and went down to the lobby. I told the man at the front desk that I had paid the room for a week, but I've decided I was only going to stay three days, and could he please refund my money for two days back. He said, "The man said don't give you the money!" I said, "Fuck the man, it's my room!" He said it again. I reached across the counter grabbed him in his chest and said "give me my goddamn money. He was looking past me shaking his head. I

LOST AND TURNED OUT   ~83~

turned around to see what he was staring at. Chicago was standing in the door of the hotel with money in one hand, holding on to Hassan's car seat in another. I was so ashamed. I felt it only for a moment because I know if that man had of gave me that money I was going to buy some crack. I let go of the clerk and turned towards Chicago he said "I was only going to the ATM you know I wouldn't have left you without any money. I could see the astonishment in his face, like he didn't know it was this serious. All of a sudden I got mad and told him to give me my baby. I was trying to snatch the car seat out to his hand. Chicago is very shy and hates making scenes in public. So he said let's go back upstairs. When we got upstairs I went in the bathroom to run me some bath water, Chicago came in behind me and closed the door then said, "If I had of known that you were going to do this to this children I wouldn't have never helped you get them out of foster care. With tears in his eyes he grabbed my head and pushed it down in the water and said, "If you want to die. I'll help you die because that's all you're doing every time you smoke that shit." He let me go and I sat on the floor and cried. After I had bathe and got myself together I told him to let's go we were going with him.

Once we got to Alex city Chicago asked me if I needed to stop at the store and get anything. I told him yes, something's for my hair. He never asked for the change back so I never mentioned it. He asked "Are we staying in Alex City tonight? Or are we going back?" I said we are going back. That money was burning a hole in my pocket. We dropped the baby off and stayed for about an hour. Then we headed back to Birmingham. I was trying to think of a lie to tell once we got back to the hotel, so I could go get some dope for the last time, because tomorrow I was on my way to treatment. After we got upstairs I told Chicago I needed to go get Anthony and Patricia's clothes from Centerpoint and my iron. He said okay. That he was tired and he'd stay here with the twins. I had ninety dollars in my pocket. I decided to stop in Norwood at the jook joint to buy me two rocks. I pulled up to the house a friend of mine was standing outside, and I bought three rocks. I smoked two and gave her one. I got my iron then headed over to Centerpoint. I got the twins two new outfits, and had all intentions of going straight back to the hotel. Sis walked in as I was walking out of the house. I said, "You got something?" She said "yeah." I said, "Give me six dimes." Now that I had the dope I was going to stop one more time and smoke with my friend. When I looked at the clock it was 8:00 pm. When I left the hotel it was 6:30 pm I thought "I better leave now." I was getting ready to get in the car when I seen the iron and children clothes on the seat. I popped the trunk to put the stuff back there when I seen two crown royal bags. I looked inside the bag. I was stunned. There was so much gold and diamonds in there I thought I had hit the lottery. Immediately the cunning and scheming began. I forgot all about Chicago, the twins, everything. The only thing that I could think about was smoking. I said to myself that I would only take two or three pieces out to sell. Shit! I and my friend went to every dope house in the bottom. Then we picked up a guy friend to take us to the dope houses we missed. We kept smoking and smoking. J.C. said, "Toni I don't want no more, you need to drink something so you can calm down." I told him that he could get out of my motherfucking car if he was through getting high.

Other crack heads loved getting high with me because I was known for being really generous. But I think this night was really too much for them. Also every dope house I went to bought the jewelry because they knew I always had paper, and always had good merchandise. When I finally slowed down a little it was day light. I still had a few more pieces left, I went to another dope house and told them I wanted an eight ball, they told me to go back to the bottom and her son would bring it to me. About thirty minutes later he did.

Need I say the sun was all the way up now? I put my friend and J.C. out of the car on the boulevard. Now, I remembered that Chicago and the kids were at the hotel. I couldn't go back there because he was going to kill me, there was no way I could go get the kids and I was driving his Lexus. I was on the freeway driving behind an eighteen wheeler. I thought if I just crash into the truck this shit will all be over. God wasn't through with me yet. I had one last alternative. I got off on 20th street Ensley to go to the rehab hoping that my old counselor would be there. I pulled the car up all the way on the curb, went to the door and I could just imagine how I looked. I was crying so hard she couldn't understand anything that I was saying. When I calmed down I told her what I had done. She told me "Toni you have to call Chicago and tell him where you are, and to get your children." When I called the hotel Ole girl answered the phone she said, "You are so low down Toni! Why, did you leave this man up here with these kids knowing that he didn't have any transportation?" I could also hear what she was not saying. She had found out that I sold all that jewelry to all the dope boys in the bottom, and didn't come to her. She brought Anthony and Patricia to me and when they saw me they just ran in and hugged me. Chicago came in and stood in front of me. I couldn't even look up, I was so ashamed. He said "my jewelry is gone, did you sell my car phone too?

My counselor told him he had to go get Hassan and bring him to me. He said okay. Then he told me that he was going to get the baby and bring him back. He said after that do not call or contact him because he was tired, and that I didn't realize how many people I was hurting. I immediately got defensive. How the fuck am I hurting anyone? Doesn't anybody give a fuck about me! Even today I noticed my daughter and son protectiveness over me. If they sense danger they surrounded me. Anthony in the front Patricia in the back, and that's exactly what they did that day.

Chicago left and came back the next morning with my baby, milk, and pampers he even brought me a color television to put in my room. He gave me three hundred dollars and told me he was washing his hands of me. He left to go back to New York. Chicago's love for me ran deep. I knew he didn't mean what he was saying, he was just mad. I don't know if it was because of the baby or if it was just me. Because even after that incident he called me everyday and let me vent while I was kicking that shit. When I got my first furlough he flew to Birmingham, paid my lawyer and took me and the kids to Alex City for the weekend.

My mom lived about five miles from me. She never came. I noticed that when I seem to be getting my shit together she never would show up. But when I failed she'd be the first one on the scene. She seen herself in me, and I think she knew I was stronger than she ever would be. I did for mine what she could never do for and me sister. I knew in my heart that I'd find a way out of my mental prison sooner or later as long as I had hope I knew I wanted to stop living like that, but I just had to find a way. For the next two months Chicago would fly down and spend my furlough time with us. I had also found out that Sean was in jail, so in between time I would go visit him at the County. We wrote each other a lot we even talked about getting back together. In my last month at the rehab it was time to look for me an apartment; this was my second phase of being clean and on my own.

Chicago's brother-in-law worked at a furniture store in Alex City. They had made a deal on my front room, bedroom, and kitchen furniture that he would deliver to me once I found my apartment. My graduation was December 14, 1994. I ended up having to move out a week early because they needed my area for another mom and kids. I found me an apartment on Fountain Heights. It was a two bedroom and that was perfect for me and my children. I only planned on being there six months to a year until I was being able to get on my feet. Chicago, western unioned me the money for two months rent and a deposit. The day I moved in his brother-in-law and a friend of his drove from Alex City to bring the furniture. I was proud of my place. It would be the first time in twenty seven years that I had my own place, paid bills, and I was really happy.

I graduated from treatment that following week. My counselors told me that if I ever needed them for a ride to a meeting, to talk, whatever they would be there. I had made a few friends so it was truly a tearful moment. One of the steps of my treatment was to make amends to people I had hurt and to the people who had hurt me, I had to find forgiveness because that was one only way that I would get well. Well, over the years W.C.had stopped drinking. I got the courage to let him know that I had hated him for what he stole from me, but I could forgive him today knowing the things I had learned. That he had been an alcoholic and a very sick man, and for me not to forgive him would keep me sick. I let him know I could never trust him around my kids by himself. Although, I forgave him. I was hurting so bad inside. I had lost so much and couldn't ever get it back. I was constantly trying to figure out why I was chosen for this journey. I did not ask for it, and it wasn't fair.

To me once a predator always a predator. Ironically, he was the one who took me to all my appointments and any errands that I needed to run. I only had a week before Christmas so I asked Chicago would he send me some money to buy my kids some things. And he did. I bought a miniature Christmas tree to sit on the table; it had the little Christmas lights. I went to the dollar store and bought the twins like tens toys a piece and Hassan some stuffed animals. Once I finished wrapping the toys and turned my tree on, it was the most beautiful tree I had ever seen, and I cried with joy because I was clean, I had my children and they would have a nice Christmas.

I took joy in keeping my little apartment clean. I didn't have to answer to anyone. Anthony didn't take to Hassan that well, but Patricia loved him to death. That was her baby. She use to call him Smiley face and he would laugh so hard. I kept in touch with a few girls from the halfway house, but after a while it was too overwhelming. Shit! I thought I had issues it was nothing compared to theirs. Chicago would call me every morning and every night to make sure we were alright. I got the impression that as long as I was by my self he would take care of me. I learned that if you let another person control your destiny, then you lose yourself also. Over the years I learned to take care of myself and at that moment I felt I had no one in the world but me and my kids. I was lonely and missed companionship. All of the friends I had either smoked dope or used it and I was determined to keep my sobriety.

About two days after Christmas, I noticed the light on my phone blinking. I had a message. The message said, "Hey, Toni this is Bro call me." I'm trying to search my mind and figure out who the Bro was. The next message was the same but this time he added he was a girl I had went to elementary school with, brother. I had dated her brother when I was fourteen. I called the number he left; he answered the phone and told me that he had got my number from my mom baby brother when they were in prison together. Bro had just come home December 7th, 1994. He asked me where I lived, I told him. He said once he got a ride he'd be over. I went about my business and had completely forgotten about the call. I started my dinner; my kids loved spaghetti so that's what I was making that night. I heard a knock at the door. When I opened it, it was Bro I looked in his face and it all rushed to my brain about how in love I was with this boy. It felt just like it was yesterday, it had actually been thirteen years. We talked as I cooked and laughed about all the stuff we did back then. My dinner was finished. I fed the twins, and Hassan, I asked Bro if he was hungry then fixed him a plate. While he ate I bathe the kids and put them in bed.

I was very impulsive. I never thought about shit until I did it by then it would be too late. Bro ended up staying that night. He had a job working in a warehouse. His friend would pick him up every morning. I had completely forgotten about the fact that I was dating this guy named Chris who was really nice to me and my children, Sean was calling from jail and Chicago still called twice a day. But I was lonely, and I wanted someone to need me.

At first I told Bro not to answer my phone. Then after a while I was fuck it. But I was skeptical about Chicago. Then I said fuck him too. He was living with a woman so why should I be by myself. Besides, I was in love again. One of the don'ts after a person leave treatment is to abstain from relationships for a year. Definitely for me because I fell in love fast and end up getting hurt even quicker. It was just my luck that all three dudes called in the same night. Chris called first, and Bro answered the phone, he told Chris not to call anymore. Chris told him to let me tell him that, I got on the phone and told him. Then Sean called a little later from jail. This one was a little more difficult because I really cared for Sean and for three months while I was in treatment he wrote to me encouraged me, and he and Bro knew each other personally. Bro accepted the call. He told him the same thing he said to Chris. I got the phone and Sean said, "Toni you don't have to be scared of this nigga!" I told him I wasn't and that I was doing what I wanted to do. Then the one I dreaded the most Chicago said,

"Who is that nigga just answered the phone?" I said my man. You could hear the surprise in his voice. At that moment I resented him very much it was cool for him to have somebody but not me. I said, "yeah, my man!" He said that he would send money for Hassan at the first of every month and hung up.

I got a job at Sheraton Hotel downtown in housekeeping and I really liked my job. My auntie would watch the kids for me while I was at work. After a while I had me a little hustle going on. I completely quit my job because the paper was flowing. I told Bro he could even quit his job. Yeah, I was balling! Once my friend Sara found out that Bro was living with me she freaked the fuck out. She was like, "Why do you have that nigga staying in your house?" I told her that we were together. She said you didn't hear about him killing that girl in Norwood Park? I told her "No!" Then she said he beats on all the bitches he had. I didn't have enough sense to be scared. I asked him later on that night about what Sara said. He told me that "the bitch is lying!" He said, Sara knew that he knew her when she was getting high. He said one night they were at Sara's mama house and she told him she would give him some head for a rock. Anyway the danger for me is doing what people said I shouldn't do. Then I told him "You said you didn't do it so I'm cool with that, but if you ever hit me and lay down it was over, and I'd cut his ass from A-Z."

My mama claimed she didn't like him, and she hadn't even met him yet. Sara had stopped driving me to work because Bro said he would do it. You never seen us unless you seen all of us together, the kids too.

In February of 1995 Chicago called me and said he wanted to come get Hassan. He said that he and his girl were coming together. Chicago was really spiteful this wasn't about Hassan; he just wanted me to know and see his girl. I was like "You can come but you better not bring that bitch with you!" You could tell that she was in the car with him because he was trying to showboat. He said, "If she can't come I ain't coming. I said, "Cool" Bro had a court date February, 8th me, him and the kids went to court and he got a continuance. We were all dressed in Nike sweat suits that day. About two days before that Bro had mentioned that he wanted to get a dope sack. I told him "you know I can't sell it from the apartment right?" He said "yes!" He said he talked to one of his friends about it, and it was cool to sell from his house.

During the day Bro would go to Norwood and he would sell the dope out of the jook joint. Usually I didn't go with him when he went, but this was a Friday night he wanted me to go with him because it was jumping.

Around seven or eight o'clock everyone started showing up. After a while Bro told me that he was going to North Birmingham to the liquor store. He asked me if I wanted anything back I told him yes, some Bacardi Breezers. Before he left out he handed me a ziplock bag full of dope and his gun and walked out of the door. I started sweating immediately, felt like the dope was burning a hole in my purse. Then I told myself "you should have gave it back to him" Knowing I wasn't strong enough to be put in that position. I looked in my purse again and I said "If I just get one out, and act like someone bought it from me, put the ten dollars in the bag, he won't know. So I called my friend over and asked her did she have a stem. She said "yes." She gave it to me, I gave her a rock. We went in the back and I smoked it.

Now, I'm scared like a motherfucker, I told my friend "Bro is going to know that I smoked this." She said, "No he ain't! So calm down, "here drink this beer. "She said. As soon as Bro came in the door I said "I want to go home" He said "What's the matter?" I said nothing I just want to go home. He asked his friend if J.C. could borrow his car to take me home he said yes. I told J.C. that he had to stop by my Auntie house so I could pick up Hassan. Anthony and Patricia were already at home.

My friend Trina was watching them. While we're driving back to the house I asked J.C. if he had a stem. He said "yes" I said "here's twenty dollars and two rocks, let me have it. He gave it to me and dropped us off at home. I told J.C. go straight back to Norwood don't stop. I had about six rocks on me that I had taken out of the bag. So I could smoke once I got to the house.

About thirty minutes after I got home Bro called and asked me where was J.C.? I said "What the fuck you asking me for?" and hung up. He called back again and said, "I'm on my way home." I sat at my kitchen table and just cried, four months of sobriety gone just like that. I got up to go call me to see if I could come back. Before I could dial the number Bro came in the door. He came in the kitchen and asked me what was wrong? I told him I smoked some dope and I need to call my counselor. He grabbed me and said, "No, Toni, no what about the children?" He was crying and rocking me. Then he asked me where did I get the stem from? I told him J.C., but it wasn't his fault. I asked him for it. He calmly pushed me back, pulled all the phones out of the plug he said "I'll be back." I said, "Bro, please leave it alone it wasn't his fault, it was my decision. I need to go back to treatment!" He just looked at me and walked out the door. The kind of doors I had you would have to have a key to get in or out. He took my keys and locked me, Trina, and the kids in the house. I looked in the room my children was still sleep. It was so unreal it was like I had lost my motherfucking mind. Soon as he left I pulled the other rocks out and smoked them with Trina. Trina was supposed to be my babysitter but I use to kick it with her in '94, but O'Dawg didn't know that.

An hour or two later Bro came back home plugged in the phone, dialed a number. I heard him say "Is that nigga dead? I shot him dead in his chest." I bugged the fuck out. I was screaming "why did you do that? He didn't do nothing wrong! It was me! He told me to get off of him he had to leave in case the police came. He said he'd be back so wait for his call. This shit was spiraling out of control. I sent Trina to get me some more dope. I thought if I'm high I won't feel shit. Before the night was over with I had sold all my jewelry. It was pathetic. I thought if I could smoke enough crack all this shit would go away. I had lost it. Trina looked after the children because I did know if it was night or day and all I could think of is that this nigga done shot this boy! What if he died I just couldn't take it. I was so in love with this nigga, he was gone, I didn't know where he was, and he told me he'd call when he figured this shit out. What about me? Who was going to help me figure it out? When I realized all my jewelry was gone I started sending Trina to sell my designer purses, anything that I thought would sell. Bro came home the following evening he said he needed a change of clothes. He was talking to me then all of a sudden he said "Where the fuck is your jewelry? I said I sold it. He looked at me and said you are pitiful. Then he left. What was the sense in going on? I had completely forgotten about the kids. I looked up on my dresser and there was a bottle of Tylenol PM. I got the bottle, went in the kitchen, got a beer, then sat on my bed and took every last pill in one bottle. I remember waking up, each time I woke up it was different people standing over me. I heard Trina crying saying Dawg wake up. I got up one time because my mouth was so dry to get me some water. I picked up a bottle of polish remover and drunk that. Trina said I woke up another time, put on mix matched shoes to go out the door. I stayed out of it for five days. When I realized I was still here I cried like a goddamn baby.

Trina noticed that I was up and brought me food and something to drink. I got up looked in my children's room. Their room was spotless. While I was knocked out Trina took care of them really well. I just went in there and lie in Patricia's bed with all three of them and cried. I was in so much despair, I didn't know where to go, didn't know what to do, nothing. I got up later to take me a bath. I just couldn't stop crying. Bro called several times, to see if I was alright. The apartment started closing in on me, so

I got my kids dressed and we went to his mama's house. He called again once got there and asked me had the police been around I told him that they hadn't. He told me to stay on down there until the evening, and then go home, he was coming home tonight. He came home that night and he hugged, and rocked me telling me everything was going to be alright.

Two weeks after Bro had been home, he and I were lying in our room watching the stories, and the children were in the other room. The police came and took him out in handcuffs, read him his rights, and told him that he had been charged with attempted murder. For shooting J.C. that night at the jook joint.

I flipped out again. My was nigga gone. How was I going do this shit by myself? I always felt that I needed someone, even when I knew deep down inside they weren't no good. I was okay with them just being there.

Never thinking I had so much more to live for and three of them were in the back room. I called Trina to come over. I went on a crack spree. I couldn't face what was going on, didn't think enough of myself to know I didn't need a nigga to survive. I found out that Bro had a ten thousand dollar bond, and he had about two or three holds on him at the city. He would send his sister over to pick me up and I would hide in the bath room because I was too shame for them to see me. He kept calling the house, asking me what was wrong. Half of the time I couldn't come to the phone because I was paranoid. I didn't even care anymore. I was just, existing. I did the best I could with the kids. Hell, I had stopped going outside, if I did go out it would be at night. I would sleep all day and my children would sit in there until I woke up, and sometimes Patricia would come in my room on her own, change Hassan, get his bottle, put some milk in it, and then take him in the room with them.

My mama called told me that she could hang out with her. All our clothes were dirty so I got up and washed two outfits for them to wear the next day. Besides all our clothes with tags on them I had sold. I had to wash me something out too because I was going to go to work the next day. That night I let Sara's son come up to my apartment so he could bag his dope up. When he finished he gave me the plate with a lot of crack on it and left. I said to myself before I start getting high let me feed, bathe, and put my children to bed first. That's what I did. I had sold all the televisions except the one in the children's room. I just stayed in the house with my front door open looking out my storm door.

After, a while I left out of the front room and went into my bedroom. I must didn't realize the amount of dope I put on the stem because the next thing I knew, I thought I heard someone outside my door saying "kill that bitch when she come out" I hit the floor and crawl to the kitchen and got three knives out, went into my children's room, woke them up, gave them a knife, told them in a low voice if anyone come in cut them. I know my poor four year old children were scared out of their minds. I must have kept them on the floor for about two hours.

When I finally calmed down and turned the lights on my daughter was looking at me like I had lost my damn mind. She asked me if she could get her brothers and go into the other room. I yelled at God that night, I cried, I begged "God, if you are there and you hear me Lord, please, please take the taste of this dope out of me! I can't go on anymore Lord, my children don't deserve it. Amen." I got up went to the bathroom and flushed the rest of the dope down the toilet got in the bed and slept like a log.

I didn't feel heavy hearted that morning I felt good. After I got everybody off where they needed to go I headed to Irondale. I got arrested that day. May 15, 1995. It was the last day that I had ever smoked crack again.

I could not manage my life alone. I had tried that road and failed. My ultimate sin, dragged me down to the lowest level that I had ever reached and unable to even function. I accepted the fact that I desperately needed help; I stopped fighting and surrendered entirely to God. Then a sense of peace came over me and, I remembered the prayer I had prayed the night before. It was done! I was taken to jail, and the following week I went before judge. He let me know that he had done the best that he could do to help me. I was sentenced to fifteen years, at Julia Tutwiler Prison for women. Because my charges were non violent, I could apply for work release or any other program they had there. What made it difficult though is I found out I was two months pregnant therefore I wouldn't be eligible for anything until after I had my baby. Bro had gotten out of jail. He let the apartment go and sent Hassan to Alexander City to his grandparents. My mama had Anthony and Patricia. He was very angry that I didn't visit him in jail, so that was his excuse for not visiting me. Regardless of that he didn't even think about that I had stood by him when he got out of prison. I didn't have any friends because I had alienated all of them because of him. The bottom line was when I told him I was pregnant he said "how do I know it's mine? I decided it really didn't matter any way; it wasn't like he was going to stand by me. The hurting part was I was still in love with him. If I were honest with myself, I'd say that Bro was really the only man that I had truly genuinely been in love with as much as I could in my own way. I was transferred to prison September of 1995.

I got to Tutwiler, once I and other inmates had showered, we were placed in dorm seven until all the test had been done showing that I didn't have any kind of diseases. I stayed in dorm seven for three weeks, and then I was moved to dorm eight where pregnant, older, and sick and shut in females were. Due to me being pregnant the prison made sure that I and other pregnant inmates went to outside doctors. I found out on my first visit that I was carrying another set of twins and that they were due in October. I had a very bad disposition so anything anybody said got on my nerves. One night I got into an argument with another pregnant girl, I told her that I wasn't going to stand there and argue back and forth with her. The next thing I know she jumped up in my face and said "Bitch, Kiss my Ass!" I had a soda and a cup of hot soup in my hand. I threw the hot soup, sat down and smoked me a cigarette while she was hollering. The officers came in and I was escorted to segregation. I was let out after three days, then given thirty days restriction. I couldn't talk on the phone, go outside, have visits or go to commissary. As the days went by it got hotter and hotter. I got miserable and big as a damn house. September came, and I had to go see the doctor now every week. I was considered high risk because I was having twins. On one of my trips to the hospital, I had to stay overnight. The security company that the prison contracted with sent a security to stay with me over night. Everyone called her Lefty. Lefty ended up taking care of me through my entire pregnancy. I didn't care anything for her either, but I needed some benefits and again I had to do what I had to do. It was what I knew. Use or be used.

On October 31, 1995 at 9:04 Lee came into the world, and at 9:08 his sister, Cadesia preceded him. They weighed six pounds apiece and they were gorgeous. I was so excited and amazed that I had, had another set of twins. But the depression set in because my babies wouldn't be going home they would be going to DHR. I didn't know how much more of this world I could take. DHR which is the Department of Human Resources were going to pick them up and put them in foster care. Because my mom said she wasn't taking care of any babies, and she already had two of my children. I know that she didn't owe me anything, but I resented that lady more than ever at the time. How a person in a sound frame of mind could, let their grand children go to strangers? She only needed to watch them for me for two months. Then I would have been home to care for them myself. I never thought that I could hate a person as much as I did my mom at that time. I would have swam an ocean for her. What was I to do, what was I to say? The whole five days my leg was cuffed to the bed. I had just had a C-section, where the fuck was I going? After I got back to the prison five days later. I called my mama and asked her to call when it was convenient for her, to see who had my children. Come to find out that an older lady who was a foster parent in Bessemer had them, and they were calling my children Randy and Raven. I really had to get out of prison before I had a nervous break down.

One day my friend Ann told me that her mother in law Nap wanted to talk to me. I called her. I remember Ms. Nap from years ago and she was a very nice lady. She asked me if I wanted her to get my children until I came home. She said she knew how it felt to be away from your kids. She said she thought I'd feel better if somebody I knew had them.

Arrangements were made for her to get them, and one good part was she stayed across the street from my mama. Already Anthony, Patricia, and Hassan were visiting every second Saturday in one month. The prison had a program called A.I.M. Aid to Inmate Mothers and they allowed the mother's to interact with their children for at least four hours. The volunteers from counties all over Alabama would drive them down in a van and then take them back home. All the girls in the program were truly grateful. I know I was, because without them I wouldn't have had a way to see my kids. My mom made sure that my children were on the van every month and Big Mama brought Hassan to see me regularly. Big mama was awesome. I loved her so much because she never judged me, and she never stopped my son from seeing me. Even when I and her son weren't together.

After my six week check-up I was sent to EMC which was a minimum Camp for women that had minimum custody and could go out in the community to work. I was also able to take passes and furloughs. I was transferred down there a week before Christmas. The same day I got there Lefty brought me all kinds of jeans, shoes, and a whole bunch of things.

I worked at Montgomery courthouse and on my lunch breaks Lefty would meet me at the cafeteria. I took my first pass the following week and Lefty picked me up, she took me shopping, I cooked dinner for her, and before you knew it my eight hours were up. Lefty was a big help to me. I really appreciated all she was doing. But she wanted me to move to Montgomery once I got out. She had two children and they were both grown. At any rate I didn't think I was ready to make a move like that. We just decided we would talk that later, but as far as I was concerned that conversation was over.

I found out that a lot of females at the Camp was using, and selling drugs down there. They were being sent back to prison for dirty urine like it was the thing to do.

I hung out with this girl named Renee, and a girl I was kicking it named Paulette when I wasn't working or at home. Both of them drunk alcohol and for life the of me I couldn't understand why a person would want to be drunk or high in jail, then have to make sure you don't get caught. Renee and a few others were stealing shit out of stores every time we went shopping. One of the officers had already pulled me to the side and said that someone had come to him and said we were in a gang. I was like I don't even know what a gang does. He said I'm just telling you.

The Friday came that I was to take my furlough, Big Mama and Hassan was coming pick me up and I was going to stay in Alex City until Saturday morning, then go to Birmingham the next day. After Big Mama picked me up we went straight to the house to wait for Chicago's call. Even though he had a girlfriend whenever he could holla he would. He had also been sending me money the whole time. Big Mama's house was always cozy and toasty to me. I laid on the day bed with Hassan chilling waiting for his dad to call. The phone rang, I answered. A male voice said, May I speak to Tonithia Foster? I said this is she. He said, this is the sergeant from EMC you need to come back to the center. By that time Chicago's mom had got on the phone. She asked him if she brought me back would I be able to come back home? He said yes. Now, I'm tripping the fuck out because I didn't know what was going on. We got back to the center and the officer told me to step into the shift office. He said that they had notification from the commissioner to send me back to prison. I asked why? They couldn't give me an answer they just told me to pack my stuff. I told Big mama to go ahead because I didn't want Hassan to see that.

By the time Renee came in from work they were already walking me up to the prison. About thirty minutes later she came. I was thirty eight hot. Couldn't anyone tell me why I was going back to prison, and I didn't have a disciplinary so I needed to know something. I called Lefty and told her to call downtown to the commissioner's office and see would they tell her something, and to no avail. I asked my classification officer, she didn't know anything. In April of 1996 we got a new Warden at Tutwiler. Everyone said he was fair and that everyday at 3:00 he had an open door policy. Around the second week in April I put my name down to see the Warden. I told him my problem. He called my classification officer and asked her why I hadn't been signed up for work release. Said she didn't think it was time. He told her that she wasn't being paid to think and if we were eligible for work release then she needed to sign us up.

I got shipped to Birmingham work release on May 29, 1996. I was ecstatic. The work release was on 25th Street and my grandmother's house was on 33rd. A lot of girls I knew broke me off as soon as I got there. I told Paulette once I started working I would send her money. My birthday was that Saturday coming up and I told my mama and Nap all the food I wanted cooked, collard greens, macaroni & cheese, chicken, a whole soul food feast. The day of my visit I was called downstairs early. I didn't think that they would be that early, but I didn't care I just wanted to see my children. I burst thought the door and to my surprise, Bro and five of his sisters were standing there.

They had some goddamn nerve. My babies were eight months old, and they were just now seeing them. If I would have done and said what I wanted to, I probably would have gone back to prison that day. Oh, my God! As if it wasn't already bad, here comes my mama, Nap, and the children. While they're bringing the food in Bro and all his sisters were starring at the babies like they just couldn't believe it. Those two he couldn't deny even if he tried. He asked me if he could hold them and there were tears coming out of his eyes. He asked me when he could see them. Nap, said never! She was so funny.

Nap was sixty years old and real jazzy, and she said what she meant. I told her he was their father, but the only way he could see them was to be supervised. Bro and his sisters left, we ended up having a very good visit. I ate like I was homeless. In the prison the inmates basically the same thing every day, processed food.

My friends were coming to the side door getting food. It was so much. My visit finally came to an end, I hugged everybody I'd see them next Saturday on pass. Nap was my sponsor, and she's one that came and got me for passes.

I started out driving the van my first few weeks there. The job specialist got me a job working at the auction in Pell City. After a couple of weeks it was discovered that some of the girls from the center were getting high and having sex in the cars. They were scared that I and another girl that worked with us were going to tell. I told them I didn't give a fuck what they did; just don't bring it around me. Ironically, the supervisor called me and her in the office; he said he had to let us go because he had too many workers. The job specialist said she wasn't going to write us up for being fired because she knew some shit was going on out there. I went to the job specialist and explain my situation to her. I told her that I had five children and I needed a job that was going to pay me some money. She got me a job at DHR, on the front desk. My job was to answer phone, file, and notify social workers when their clients came in.

I called Chicago to see if he could send me some business clothes. He was good at picking out women things and if he picked it, it was going to be sharp. Over the weekend he sent me five outfits to my mama's house. She called me at work with her nosy ass and said, I opened your package. Chicago sent you some bad shit! The lowest outfit cost eight hundred dollars. By her being money hungry this really impressed her.

The job I had was something that I enjoyed. Dealing with people all the time. I also enjoyed it because if anybody wanted to see me all they had to do was come to DHR. One of the rules from work release for my job, was not to leave unless we were going to lunch for our hour. A lot of times no matter where you worked the other employees felt that they had a right to give the girls from work release orders. The first week I was there I had to check a female. She yelled at me for something really minute. The bottom line was that the job I had she wanted, and I was making more money than her. I told her first of all don't yell at me, if she wants respect she had to respect me, if she had an issue with me the chain of command was my supervisor, the center. I never had a problem again. The social worker that was handling my case worked there. She was always nice about any questions I had. My life was pretty full now. I worked two jobs; I went home every other weekend for 36 hours, played softball. I drove the van when I wasn't working. This was really good for me because it kept me busy.

A lot of females were drinking and getting high. My main objective was working and making as much money as I could. My selfishness hurt a lot of people, who really cared about me, but I wasn't ready for a relationship at that point, and I let them know that off the top. I, my mom and my sister were all living together in West end. We had a nice little house, all three of us had our own rooms, and the kids had there's. Bro was still around but I was really getting sick of him. I loved him true enough but he wasn't bringing anything to the table. He definitely had to go. At that time I was seeing two guys and a female. One of the guys worked with me. He was a social worker, and a single parent raising two daughters. The other guy was a big time drug dealer, his family owned restaurants, fought pit bulls. We met one day when he came to report his wife for neglecting his son. K.J slipped me his number and it was on. He didn't pressure me, he broke me off real proper every time I seen him. He said that every time he asked me if I need anything I said no. but if he wanted to buy something he could for my five children. He said he admired that in me. I told him I can get my own hair and nails done, just keep the paper coming. The female was really sweet. I just wasn't feeling her and even though I expressed that to her she kept coming.

After I got clean. I promised myself regardless of what the situation that I would always be honest with telling people how I felt. That way I wouldn't feel guilty about anything.

December of 1996 rolled around and everyone was getting ready for Christmas. I put in for a furlough and got approved for a week. Chicago was supposed to bring Hassan up for Christmas Eve. I asked him if he wanted me to come get him he said, no.

I made plans to go to the new club with Bro, I told him to pick me up around ten. Chicago got to Birmingham around four. He called to me to let me know they had made it. I said okay, it would only take me about ten minutes to get there. Hassan saw me before I saw them. I heard him say "there go my mama!" He ran to hug me, then Chicago got up greeted me then hugged me.

I thought that he was going to leave once I picked up Hassan, but he told me he wanted to see the other kids. He followed me out to my house. When we got into the house he hugged and kissed all my children. I was really anxious for him to leave because I didn't want Bro and him to have words. Bro had already called several times since I had been back in the house. My mama with her phony self spoke to Chicago as he walked in "Hey Chicago, how's my son-in-law doing?" I was standing behind him trying to get her to stop talking to him so he could go on.

All in all we had a really good Christmas. January of 1997 rolled around and with it the cold weather. Things were looking pretty good for me. I had signed up for a program called SIR; it was like parole, except a better structure which was okay with me. I just wanted to go home. I had a very good chance at making it. I didn't have any disciplinarians, and the people at work had given me good reports. All I was waiting on was an approval from Montgomery. The second week in January, I got a call from my social worker in New York. She wanted to know if I was ready to sign the adoption papers. It was going to be an open adoption meaning that, Willie's foster mom still had to deal with the court. I also wanted it stipulation that Willie would always be able to communicate with my other children. That was very important to me. My maternal side of the family had never been close. I didn't want that for my children. I needed them in case something ever happened to me, to know that they always had each other.

Thursday came and I got a call at work fro the center letting me know that my social worker and her supervisor were there. The officer was sending a van to pick me up. When I got there I was told to go into the dining room. I saw my worker first, then her supervisor. They told me to read over the papers and then sign. Before I signed I looked at worker and I told her to promise me she would let Willie know that I had done it for him so he could be happy. I was crying so hard I could hardly see the paper. I also told her I know he's going to have questions. When he's of age or even before, he could call me and I'll always be there for him. That was the hardest thing in the world for me to do. But my son had grew into that family, and I knew that they loved him very much and he them. To take him would have been very selfish of me, and hurt him. That was final. I felt such a loss. Although, I hadn't raised Willie he was still my son. No matter what anyone says, a mother will always have a connection to a child that she brings into the world.

My pass was coming up, so I was trying to prepare for that. The big twin's birthday had passed; I was going to give them a belated party. I made reservations at a place I in Hoover. Before I got ready to go out that morning my friend Renee asked me if I was going to get some money this weekend. I told her no, because I was going to have my children's party. Trice picked me up at 8:00 am Saturday morning. We ran the usual errands, and then went home. I invited my social worker friend and his two daughters.

Around 6:00 we headed out to Hoover, I remember one of my children saying mama there goes your van. One of the girls that drive the van was out there picking up the other girls from the cleaners. The party was a success; the children had a great time. I made plans to spend the night out with my friend. I let him know that my sister would drop me off as soon as I went and got the other kids settled; the twins were coming with me.

Trice dropped me off at his house around 9 p.m. I told her I'd call her in the morning to come pick me up. I spent a nice evening with him. The next morning Trice picked me up. That would be the last time I saw him. My sister pulled up outside and blew the horn. When I looked out the window I noticed someone else in the van. I thought maybe it was my mom, but the person was too big to be her. As I got closer to the van I realized that it was Renee. I asked her what she was doing in there. She said that her and her girlfriend had gotten into a fight at a hotel on 3rd avenue, and that she left walking. She said she needed to go get some money because she wasn't going back to the center; she wanted to know if I would take her stealing. My mama walked out of her bedroom looked at

Renee and rolled her eyes. I heard her tell Trice "don't give Toni my keys!" I told Renee after I ate and changed clothes I would run her out to Roebuck. She wanted to go to the Goody's.

I heard a horn blowing outside when I looked out the window it was KJ. He was driving a brand new SUV and he wanted me to see it. I told Renee if she wanted to make some money she could ask him for his children sizes and he'd buy anything that she could get. KJ and I finished our conversation he told Renee to call him once we got back. I told him I'd call him later on tonight. We left my mama's house at 12:30 pm because the stores didn't open until 1 p.m. on Sunday. We left my mom's house, me, Trice, her boyfriend and Renee.

The first store she went in, she stole maybe two pieces. The next store the same. I was getting very frustrated cause we were pressed for time. Plus we had to be back at the center at 8 p.m. I told my sister to drive to the grocery store in Pell City because Renee was taking too long to get paid. I went in the store, got a wallet there were two Sears cards and a J.C. Penny Card. Renee was supposed to go into the Sears and charge up stuff that she could sell. I told her that I was going to Penny's so she needed to hurry up, it was already 5p.m. by the time I came out of Penny's and got in the van I didn't see Renee no where I told my sister's boyfriend to run in Sears to see if he had seen her anywhere. He came back, no Renee. I was getting a very bad feeling.

We circled the mall parking lot, we still didn't see her. So I said fuck it, let's go. When we got back to my house I changed clothes and told my mama, and sister to take me back to the center. We pulled up to the center I seen two of my friends in the window telling me to go back, but I didn't understand what they were saying. I walked in and two officers were in the office. I looked down; one of them had handcuffs in her hands. She told me to turn around. My mama asked her why and the other officer who I was cool with went into detail and told us everything that had transpired from the grocery store to the mall. Only three other people knew. Two of them were outside in the van. The other upstairs in lock up. Renee had got caught shoplifting in Sears. After searching her police discovered the Sears credit card on her. They told her if she told where the card came from they'd give her a was a misdemeanor. She told them everything.

We ended up going back to prison. The Judge offered me ten years but they would have to start that day. Anything that I had served on the fifteen year sentence from 1995 to 1998 was null and void. If I didn't want to take that then the sentence would be ninety-nine years. I took the ten. In all I would end up doing three years before I got out again.

1999

Coming over from work in the clothing factory, as I'm coming through the gate Tank said, "Toni they want you in the shift office." Everybody in Tutwiler knew that Tank was the biggest liar around so I said, "Tank go head on now." She said, "Toni on Caleb, they called you." When she said that and I looked in her eyes, I knew in my soul it was true I walked down the hall in a daze. My state family beside me. Inside the shift office their were about four officers. One officer knew my mom when she was there. She said, "Foster you need to call your mom at your sister's house." I asked her, "Why? you call her." She said, "Toni, please!" I already knew deep in my soul I could feel it.

My mama asked me, "Was I sitting down?" Was someone in the shift office with me? Then she said, "She's gone!" I felt like someone had kicked me in my head. I mean after all these years, the trama, the drama, in our lives. I still loved my grandmama with all my heart. To me she had been dead a long time ago when she was diagnosed with Alzheimers, because she wasn't the strong fiesty, woman that I knew. But to know that I would never lay my eyes on her again nearly killed me. Because growing up that's who I remember mostly, Mrs. Mary A. Arnold.

I was allowed to go to the funeral. My sister paid two hundred dollars for two officers to escort me. I didn't have to be handcuffed because I was in minimum custody. When we go to Bushelon Funeral Home nobody was there. After about ten minutes people started showing up. I saw people I hadn't seen in years. My twin's father even brought hem. As usual my mama had to make a grand entrance in a stretch limosine. Then she saw me and put on her performance, she said, "Toni them motherfuckers better not say nothing to me, they killed my mama." My sister and I walked in together and we sat together. I was okay until they decided to close the casket. I couldn't breathe and then I thought my grandma couldn't breathe. I kept saying I was sorry. "I'm sorry mama. I'm sorry." I was sorry that she had to go through all the things that she had been through while she was sick, and that I wasn't there for her.

After the service the officers took me to the gravesite. We stayed there about twenty minutes. Then we headed on back to Tutwiler. I felt empty and hollow like another part of my life had passed me by. Where all the years had went? Although I felt that my grandmother knew what was going on. I found out later on that she was also a victim of molestation. In T.D. Jakes movie, Woman Thou Art Loosed, the mother states after her daughter was molested "When it happened to me, my mama said, we have our crosses to bare and our dresses to wear!" I often wondered did my grandmama know what was goin on. And by denying it, she could act like it never happened. Yet I still loved her till the end.

2000-2005

I got involved with a female that thought prison was home. People tried to tell me, but I had to see for myself. I stayed in one warden's office because this girl was like public enemy number one in there. Therefore I was guilty by association. I thought I was in love that soon turned to hate for disrespecting me and herself on a regular basis. I went to lock up five times in the three years I was there. Four of them were because of her. In January of 2000, I went down the hill to EMC; it had changed a lot since 1996. Only a few females were working no one was taking passes, and basically all we did was sit around all day. Around this time Chicago had come back in my life. He had started sending me money and all the other stuff I needed. I was really miserable at EMC.

I got into a fight and got sent back up on the hill to segregation for twenty one days. Once Base found out I was up there she would come to lock up door and say all kinds of crazy shit to me. I paid her no mind because I knew once I got back in population that other female was history. When I came out of lockout I tried to kick it with her, I realized that I didn't even want to be bothered. This prison shit was getting old and so was I.

I took a good look at all the crazy shit that was going on in the prison, and how I was involved. I kicked back, stayed in the dorm, read books, anything to stay out of trouble. I signed back up for work release in May of 2000 and sat back and waited. Chicago was sending me self help motivational books. Through the outside grapevine, I heard that Chicago was straight balling. I needed some stability and I knew all I had to do was say the word and he would be there. I was definitely leaning towards the home team.

My best friend Skeet and I had a two for one store going in our dorm, and just sitting back waiting for our decisions. This one particular day I had decided that I would go outside to play cards. On the weekends that were the thing to do, run outside to get a table and sit up and gamble all day for commissary. I went outside and my card partner, Betty asked me if I wanted to be her partner. I said cool, who else is playing? I kept feeling someone watching me but I shook that shit off and kept playing. The shift office announced over the PA system that it was a yard call. If anybody wanted to go in or come out they could at this time. I looked up and I saw Base come to the door. I had no idea that she would come to the table where we were. She stood there for a couple of minutes and said, "I heard you are supposed to be kicking it with someone in the dorm." I looked at her rolled my eyes, and kept playing. Instinct told me to turn around, but I was too late. She grabbed me by my ponytail. I fell backwards onto the ground and curled up in a fetal position. Base was stomping me in my face, my back anywhere that her feet could go. I heard my friend Trina exclaim "don't keep hitting her; you see she isn't fighting back." By that time an officer came and put her in handcuffs.

All the females that were on the yard were screaming "Toni didn't hit her back!" The main reason I didn't hit her back was I knew in my heart that she had planned it that way. She betted on me hitting her because I would have lost me work release status. This hoe was evil like that.

My face was swollen, my eye was closed shut, but my pride was hurt more than anything. I felt that I had done the right thing because I wanted to leave prison and go home to my kids.

The sergeant locked Base up that day. The warden kept her in segregation until I left going to work release. I had made it up there in time for the July 4th bar b Que. I left the center in 1997 now it was 2000 and all the officers and rules had changed. Because I had a valid driver's license I had to drive the van to take the other females back and forth to work. When I asked the new job specialist how long did I have to drive he told me that it would be anywhere from sixty to ninety days. I was really frustrated because my main reason for wanting to be at work release was to work and help my sister with my kids. I wanted immediate results, and I wanted them, now. I had a new addiction called, money.

Chicago had sent me money to the Western Union. I was violating then. Because we were only to drop off inmates at their jobs and picked them up, but that was my only source of income so I did what I had to do. The forth of July came around and the officers gave a cookout for us outside it was really nice but still not like being at home.

I made up my mind that I was going to leave. July 14, 2000. I did my runs dropping everyone off at their jobs. I stopped at a store and called Chicago. I told him that I needed him to send me a plane ticket to New

York. He told me to call him back around 11:00 p.m but before he hung up he asked me if I was sure that this is what I wanted to do. I reassured him that it was. I called him back at 11:00 he told me that my plane ticket was at the airport and that my plane left at 3:30p.m. I drove to my sister's house. I told her I had to go. She told me to just call her when I got where I was going.

I went to Englenook parked the van in front of a church and walked the rest of the way to JC's house. It had been five years since Bro had shot him. He and I were still cool regardless of what had happen and he tried to talk me out of it, he said he could and would help me. That he had always been attracted to me, but I was adamant about leaving.

I knew I needed money, and the destination I was heading in I would get it. Getting a job wasn't an option. My plan was to get a nice piece of money, retain a lawyer in Birmingham in case I got caught and also to send for my children.

I boarded that plane that evening determined to reach my goal. There was a lay over in Atlanta due to bad I didn't get to New York until about four a.m. that morning. The first face I seen when I got off the plane was Chicago. He said, "You were serious weren't you?" I said, "I'm here!" One thing about Chicago that I really appreciated was his word was bond, if he told you something he was going to do, it was done.

After we got all the pleasantries out of the way, I let him know what my plans were. I didn't come to start any problems with him and his girl. I just wanted to get me some money. Chicago lived in the Bronx. By the time we got there I was tired as hell, so I took me a shower and went to sleep on the coach. I must have been tired mentally and physically because I slept for about nine hours straight. It was still raining at by the time I got up and got myself together. Chicago introduced me to his girlfriend. Her name was Heaven, she was a stripper, and she had two kids. I could tell of the top that my presence intimidated her. I assured her that I didn't want Chicago although he was my son's father we would always be friends. I never understood where he found all these insecure week ass females.

I got me a room downtown at the Howard Johnson. Before you knew it Chicago had more clothes in my room than he had in his apartment. After a while he took Heaven and her children back to New Jersey. I had gone to work a couple of times, so I had paper. I made sure my sister had money for her and my children. My mama was living in New York too, and she and Chicago didn't get along. I would see her up on 7th avenue kicking it with other "hustlers" Chicago had a tendency for saying that he hated dope fiends, and poverty. He would always say, "The way your mama treated you, you shouldn't want to have anything to do with her." That was his way of pouring salt, to make sure I was tied to him. Anything that he thought would distract me from him he disliked. He was so busy trying to make sure he kept people from around me he never realized how loyal I was to him. Just on the strength of him always being there for me. All the females he had around him, he felt if he pitted them against each other they'd all be competing against each other. Chicago had his own issues. He was attracted to females that he had to reconstruct, that way they would be indebted to him. All the women he ever had were drug users, from the projects, or girls with low self esteem. Although, I fit all of those descriptions. I was hungry for knowledge and was learning that I really didn't need anyone. It was going to come a time when I rely grasped that concept and it was going to be awful.

One thing you needed to know about Chicago was he wasn't physically abusive. He was mentally abusive. He knew that I still loved my mom and my sister no matter what. To him that was not acceptable. He needed to have my mind constantly on him. So he made it his business to remind me of my past and the things my mom didn't do. And for awhile I let him brain wash me into believing he was all I wanted or needed by letting me know the things he did for me and my children. I felt like if he could have paid someone to keep my kids away from me he would have. But he fucked up and let me think too long. I told him one day that he acted just like a bitch, always repeating things other people had said. And constantly keeping up confusion with his female friends, and me. I decided regardless of what happened in my past she was still my mom, and I let him know if I stopped affiliating with her, it would be because I wanted to not because he said so. He was so busy pointing out other people faults, that he couldn't recognize his own.

He thought by spreading money around, he made friends, what he didn't know was as soon as the money ran out so did the friends, as he would soon find out.

I didn't give a fuck what he said junkie or not she was still my mother. I had been gotten over her treatment of me as a child, or so I thought.

I realized that, that was who she was and if she had not changed in all these years she wasn't going to. I dealt with her on my time. Christmas of 2000, I sent for my children, and Chicago's daughter, it was out of the question for me to go to Birmingham because I was on escape, so they came to me. Days before it was time for them to leave we all came down

TONI SHEALEY

with the flu. They went back to Alabama the day after Christmas. The other children left the day after New Year's.

After the holidays I was really getting paranoid about being in that apartment. Because all of Chicago's ex-females knew that I was there and on escape. When I mentioned he would say "they are cool", and Heaven does what I tell her to do!" He had a whole lot to find out about females. In February, Chicago, and two of his friends took a trip to Minnesota. I really didn't trust his ex girlfriend and Chicago together at all. He told me she said that he should have told her he was still in love with me when they were together. She was still a little salty about that, but stunting around me like she was cool. I dropped Chicago off at the Airport.

Before he left we knew that it was a blizzard over there, so it was going to be kind of hard for them to find rooms. But he like working in this kind of weather, because he said only people that is out is people taking care of business. I told him "if you get over there and you and your ex have to share a room let me know so it won't be any surprises!" He said "okay" while he was gone I hung out downtown in my friend Goldie's shop. She called it Goldie Loc's and she did natural hair only, and extensions. I would answer the phones for her and help her out until she closed. Goldie and I had met year's ago on Riker's Island when we both were pregnant. Plus, we had hung in the same circles at the Riverton. Goldie was from Brooklyn, it was something about the females that came out of Brooklyn. I believe it was because all the ones I knew had, had a lot of heart and I admired that in them. I also had run back into Mona. We went out to eat and she was curious about the children, and I asked about her daughter. One thing led to another and we ended up at her crib. I told her I needed to be honest with her about my situation, so that she would have a choice on if she wanted to go along with what I said. I let her know up front that I wasn't going to leave Chicago. That wasn't even an option. That when he's in town I wouldn't be able to be with her but when he was I could. She agreed with the plan. But after a while she started complaining about why I couldn't stay over night, why couldn't we see each other more often. It was really frustrating to me because I let her know off the top is the reason I couldn't spend the night, was because Chicago would call me on the house phone early in the morning, and around ten at night. My dumb ass had call forwarding but I didn't know how to use it.

Mona had offered to come do it for me but I didn't want her knowing where we lived in case she decided on a surprise visit. I didn't show my mom where I lived either because I didn't need that added stress I would visit her, or see her up on the avenue. A lot of times I wouldn't go see her because I hated too see her high.

One night Chicago and I was in the kitchen talking, somehow we got on the subject of junkies and Chicago said something about my mother, and before I knew what I was doing I slapped the shit out of him. He jumped up and backed me into the wall and said, "Bitch, if I don't hit you don't put your motherfucking hands on me." Then he said "As a matter of fact get out of my house." Of course I didn't go anywhere. Everything just went back to normal. The only thing was Chicago was a handsome man, and he had a lot of things going for him but he was in denial about a whole lot of things. I would be the one to point them out. I asked him "wasn't it strange that the only females you messed with came from dysfunctional families, used drugs at some point, had been involved with other women, and had just got out of the penitentiary? I never got an answer from him; I assumed it was because any other type of woman intimidated him. He needed to be in control at all times. For each person he critized, he had one of each in his family. A junkie, a lesbian, a mental patient and an alcoholic but he over looked all that because he came from a family of (morals and principals) on the up side his mama (Big Mama) was a gem. Because he was her son didn't make a difference. She stood by what was right. She never sided with me or Chicago but she damn sure would let us know when we were wrong.

Chicago's first three children were from his first wife. He loved Robin, but she didn't conform to what he wanted her to be, she simply liked drugs better than she did her children. Big Mama raised all three including my son as I went in and out of prison. But she made sure I seen him and that he knew I was his mama.

I called my mama and told her that I'd be to pick her up Sunday so that we could go get our nails done, and go out to eat. I called Mona and asked her if she wanted to come she said "yes". I picked my mama up then we met Mona on 254th and Greenhill Road. While we were getting our nails done Mona waited on us. I finished first, we stepped outside to smoke. I kept looking in the shop to see what was taking my mother so long because when I left out she was just drying her nails. I walked back in the shop and seen her sitting in the back where the dryer was. That's when I noticed she was nodding, high on heroin, and had stuck her hand clean through the fan ruining her nails. It was a good thing the fan was plastic. I was so goddamn mad and embarrassed. Once she got her nails repaired. I didn't feel like going to eat, so I told Mona that I'd see her later. She jumped in a cab and my mom got on the subway. No sooner had I got home my cell phone rang. I noticed that Chicago's ex and her girl was sitting in the front room. I spoke, and then answered my phone. The man on the other end asked me if my mother's name was Patricia McCracken. I said "yes" he said she had just feel down the subway steps. I asked him was she hurt badly, he said "no" I said "okay" and hung up the phone.

I began to notice that Chicago was careless about having large sums of money around, and then he told me that his friend had a key to the apartment. This shit had gone on long enough. While he was calling these people his buddies they were constantly plotting on his ass. See as long as she was around his ex could manipulate Chicago the way she wanted to because Heaven didn't have enough sense to say anything, but then I came along and fucked up her little plan. She would call Chicago and say shit like, "that bitch is going to hurt you!" His friend because he knew that Chicago was in love with me, and he felt threatened. I asked Chicago one day was he gay? Because he had righteously start getting territorial.

The time had come for me to get back down and do my thing so Chicago planned a trip. We weren't supposed to leave until early the next morning, but I wanted to leave right then because I wasn't feeling comfortable in that apartment. We left and came back that following Friday. When we were getting ready to unlock the door a card fell out on the floor. The card was from a FBI agent and they wanted Chicago to call. He never did. We started taking more and more trips after a while we were never home. A lot of times I would just fly back to New York to put up money then fly back wherever we were at that time.

In March of 2001, we had been over in Chicago for about a month. We stayed with Chicago's brother in Dolton, Ill. This is a suburb on the Southside of Chicago. It was really pretty up there and it kind of reminded me of the south. I started pushing Chicago towards moving there. Also, Chicago has asked me to marry him in the later part of 2000, but we had a problem, his first wife wouldn't sign the divorce papers. She was on drugs really bad, Chicago told me to ask her "if he paid her thousand dollars would she sign?" Robin said "No" but two nights later she called and left a message on my pager saying to tell Chicago to call her. Any contact with his kid's mom side of the family had to be made by me; he hated these people with a passion. He would ask me time and time again, "How a woman could bring children into this world and didn't want to have any dealing with them?" But only God and Robin knew.

I had sent for Hassan and Chicago's daughter for Thanksgiving. His daughter and I hung out a lot plus she would talk to me about a lot of things she didn't with her father. She was wise beyond her eleven years and was very curious. Big Mama called me one night to tell me that Robin would be getting out of prison on Saturday, well his daughter heard the conversation, and after I hung up the phone she said, "Toni why doesn't my mom love me? You use to use drugs, but you came for Hassan?" My heart broke in a thousand pieces. I had to compose myself before I answered. I told her "that some people are sicker than others, and that her mother did love her but she had a problem and needed some help." And I told her "it's not your fault. So you keep praying for her okay?" After a while she said, "Will you take me to see my mama?" I told her "yes, I would" I pulled Chicago to the side and told him what she said, he had tears in his eyes, he got angry, he said, "That bitch doesn't deserve to see her!" I told him to put his personal feelings aside. Robin was still their mom, and no matter how much you denied it, it was true." "Let your daughter judge for herself, she'd see in time." The next day I called Robin and I asked her what would be a good time for me to bring her? She said, "Around 3:00 p.m." I told her that "that would give us time because I was taking their daughter and Hassan to the zoo. I'll call before I come."

My mama met us at the Bronx Zoo. I, she and the kids had a ball. Around 2:30 I called Robin to let her know that we were coming. I looked at their daughter and asked was she ready she said, "Yes, ma'am." We caught a taxi from the Bronx to Harlem, it took us less than ten minutes to get to 117th in the building that Robin lived in, when we got to the door Robin's mom answered the door. She immediately hugged the baby and spoke to the rest of us. Robin came out the back room. I could tell that she was nervous as she awkwardly hugged her. My son, who is very affectionate and cheerful boy, hugged everyone in the room like he had known them all his life. Robin talked to her daughter, and she responded with a lot of one word answers gave her a lot of one word answers.

My mom and I tried to lighten up the conversations with the other people in the room. I could tell that Robin was very uncomfortable and she didn't make it any easier for her. She stood her ground like a little soldier. Her confidence quietly said, "I am your daughter you missed out on my life. Your loss not mines!" I applauded her in my mind. In a couple of years this little girl would be a force to reckon with.

We left with a promise of her coming to spend the night on Friday. My mom wanted to go over to 7th avenue so we caught a cab there. I was just going to drop her over there and continue to the Bronx. But when we got around there I saw people I knew and got out to talk with them. One of them was my oldest son's father, Sonny Boy. He was getting old and it showed in his face. I still had a problem talking to him without getting angry so I moved on. I talked with a few more people, and then the kids and I left.

Unfortunately Chicago's uncle passed away. His daughter wanted to cut their trip short because she said "Big Mama needed her." So she never got a chance to spend the night anyway. My grandmama always said, "God protects babies and fools!" Chicago said when he called Robin that night from D.C. she said she would go ahead and sign the papers if he gave her the thousand dollars. Instead of going back to Chicago, we went to New York.

Chicago and I were married March 6, 2001 at Cook County Court House. We hadn't completely made the move over to Chicago because we were looking for a place. Chicago had finally decided to move so it was official we were definitely moving. Before we moved to Chicago. I tried to set up a visit with Willie's foster mother. so that Willie could visit with his other brothers and sisters. I called her house and Willie answered the phone. When he realized it was me he said "I don't want to talk to her" and dropped the phone. I asked her why he angry was. She said that Willie had sent pictures to the prison I like he always do, and that the pictures were returned back to him, torn. I told her that I didn't believe that. Because if I wasn't at the prison the mail room would "return to sender." I begged her to please tell him to come to the phone. To no avail.

I asked my attorney if she would set up a visit with the kids. She called. According her the visit was to take place that Saturday. She would pick up Willie and bring him to the designated meeting place. But wen she got to the house in Brooklyn it was empty. No sign of living inside, an empty house. She hired a private investigator to look for any clues. He reported back to her that there were no forwarding address or anything. My son was twelve the last I heard from him. I was very angry. Everyone suggested that she was scared that I would try to take him back that was the reason she ran. I pray for him every night and I have every confidence that either he'll find me, or I'll find him. Through the years I had learned how to shut out anything that affected me emotionally. I took my problems and put them in the deep recesses of my mind. Slowly but surely the anger, bitterness, and resentments were building higher, and higher, and higher.

Besides that, the work was on hold, because the material we were using wasn't working for us anymore. That's what Chicago told his friend. His ex was running her mouth saying that Chicago had changed since him and I had been together. I knew she was jealous because she thought that she and Chicago had a chance of getting back together.

I told her "Sweetie all you didn't do in the three years that you all were together won't get done." She was not happy about us being married. She said it should have been her. We finally found a nice condominium in the south suburbs of Illinois. We closed on the deal and moved in, in May 2001. Chicago left it up to me to furnish it. I sent for Anthony and Patricia at the end of May. I was so happy about them being with me. At the same time I was kind of nervous because I was still on escape, thinking that these people might pop up at any time. I started getting really bad headaches. They were so bad I had to go to a specialist to give me something for the pain. The twins started school in August 2001. They were involved in all kinds of activities. Anthony played football and Patricia was into gymnastics.

Once they started school I was left with a whole day free. Chicago had found the equipment he needed to start back working. He paid a guy a thousand dollars to teach me how to use the computer. But I wanted more than that. I wanted to be hands on because I seen the type of money that was jumping off. Chicago was adamant about that. He said I had my children up there and he didn't want to risk me being caught up. I was getting restless just sitting around the house and Chicago felt me too. He started giving me money to go downtown on Michigan Ave. to have lunch in the Water Towers. It was nothing for me to walk up in Gucci to buy a pair of shoes, purse, or a dress. Michigan Ave was our second home. Chicago feared being broke and in poverty and he made it his business to live in quality and that I did the same. My children and I never wanted for anything.

I also sent money once a month to my smaller kids in Birmingham that lived with their father's sister. After a while I went out to look for a job. I got tired of doing nothing. I got a job working as a front desk clerk at a hotel Lansing, Ill. I liked my job; it kept me busy along with being in my children's life. I took them to plays, to the Navy Pier, and the Shea Aquarium. I could tell that they were happy just to be with me and so was I with them. One night Chicago asked me to name one thing I took pleasure in doing as far as work was concerned. I told him I really liked cleaning and dealing with people. He gave me ten thousand dollars and told me to open a business. So, I thought of a name for my janitorial service. "Superior Excellence", I ran an ad in the local paper for three weeks to make sure no one else was using that name; I looked for a location, which I found in downtown Homewood, Ill. I made my own flyers and drove all around the South Suburbs passing them out. I made business cards, got insured, licensed and bonded. I joined the Chambers of Commerce. Opened a business account, and went to Sam's and bought seven vacuum cleaners. I bought seven buckets of every kind of cleaner imaginable, and hired a company to issue my checks to me and my two employees, bi-weekly. I bought, learned and mastered Quickbooks Software to help me along the way, and got my business license.

Now, I was ready for business. By going to the Chamber of Commerce meetings I was able to network and get my name out. I also acquired several clients. I sub-contracted with this guy that sold carpet. So not only did I clean, I could measure and lay your carpet on the next day. Things were looking up and I was really enjoying working. I had hired my husband's first cousin, and another female they were both punctual and reliable. Around November I was looking for something in my walk-in closet and came across a lot of information that my husband had supposedly hidden. I opened the box and a lot of information was in there. I started opening up instant credit accounts and bought all kinds of stuff Christmas. Chicago never questioned me because I spent that kind of money anyway.

January 8, 2002 I went to get some things because my twin's birthday was that day. I wanted them to have everything, plus I was giving them a party at the skating rink. I was arrested that day and taken to jail; once my fingerprints had been taken the police found out that I was wanted in Alabama for escape. Chicago was furious and my children were devastated.

I was held in Cook County jail. My attorney was, a congress woman whom Chicago fired once he found out that she wasn't doing what he asked. He hired another attorney and I ended up getting two years to be run concurrent with a 1998 case I had in Alabama. My attorney in Birmingham had the escape dismissed so I only had to do the time I stayed gone. I was extradited to Alabama back to Julia Tutwiler Prison for women in May of 2002. It seemed like I had spent most of my life in this place.

God knows I was happy because I really wanted to get this time over with. I was tired of going in and out of prison. For the next year and a half I read books, moved in the honor dorm, and got sent to the minimum Camp the last sixty days of my incarceration. I had a lot of time to look back over my life and what it had been. I knew that deep in my heart it was time for me to slow down.

My husband made sure I had every thing I needed, and I got to see my children every month. Out of the money I had on commissary I sent my children a hundred and twenty dollars of that every month. That was all we were allowed to send home.

Time doesn't stand still for anyone. Big Mama passed, and that took a whole lot out of me too. I thought that she would be around forever. That was the one thing in my life that was solid and true. She was like the mom I never had, and always wanted. Chicago came to see me all the way up till my release in October 21, 2003. I had started having doubts about him before I came home. He always tried to make me feel obligated to him. God knows I appreciated everything this man did for me and my children. He was constantly throwing that up in my face. The sex was even a turn off and I had to ask myself is this really worth all the drama and unhappiness. I wanted so bad to tell him to go to hell. But because I felt I needed him to get on my feet again. I sold myself short. The first day I got out I stayed in Alexander City with my son. The next morning we headed to Birmingham.

PBS did a Mother's Day segment on me and a few more girls and they were at the door filming my release. You would think it would have been the happiest day of my life, but I got really sick because the pollen was really high, but this man wanted to have sex and to me that was like going to a firing squad. My sister and I got into it really bad about three days later. Chicago had flown back to Chicago. I stayed in Birmingham to try and find a job and place to live.

I moved in with my friend Vee. She and I were lovers in 1994 and had dibbed and dabbed over the years. She wanted a relationship right then, but I could not focus on a relationship and my other issues at the same time. Chicago called me everyday carefully dangling the fact that if I flew up there on the weekends I could make me some money. Of course that appealed to me. Then finally I said, "fuck it" I asked Vee if would she keep the big twins, and I'll take the little twins with me to Chicago. We agreed that I'd send her money every month plus get whatever they needed. My purpose for going to Chicago was that I would find a house, and could send for the rest of my kids and stay with my husband. Every time I brought up the subject of a house he shot it down. Always having excuses why the house wasn't right. I got a job working at another hotel in Finley Park.

I also sent for Chicago's son Lil Chicago to come live with us, because he was having problems in the south. Before long he and Big Chicago started getting into it about things that Big Chicago felt was wrong. But instead of him talking to him like the young man he was, treated him like a child. I would get angry because of some of the things Big Chicago said to his son. Imposing rules on this young man like he's been in his life all the time. He sent them money true enough but Chicago's mom and dad took care of his three kids. This boy was eighteen, it was a way you needed to deal with a teenager not pull-up saying he wasn't going to be nothing, or "when I was your age I wasn't in my mama's house." Or, "I tell you what go try to stay with your mom folk in New York." Knowing the type of family that Lil Chicago mama came from. Constantly belittling the young man instead of telling him positive things. Chicago wasn't setting a good example because his kids weren't crazy they knew that all the money we had didn't come from having a nine to five.

Anthony started having problems in Alabama. I sent for him to come to Chicago so I could talk to him. He said wasn't nothing going on but I kind of felt like he was lashing out at me. I started feeling guilty because here I was, I had been out of prison for five months and I hadn't sent for them yet. The money was there, but that was just another thing to control me with. It wasn't a good idea unless my husband thought of it. I caught my self flinching every time Chicago touched me, or going in the bathroom to change clothes so he couldn't look at me. I found all kinds of porn tapes in the closet; he wanted me to take naked pictures. I asked him "why?" He said to have when I wasn't around.

We had a double king it was enough room in my bed for five adults. Yet, I had shared my past with him. He knew how I felt because I told him. He would wait until I was sleep and touch me, and I thought I would die. Then if I was watching television he would act as if he was sleep and massage his nipples. It seemed like he was obsessed with sex.

I just broke one day. I said "why in the fuck do you do that?" I told you if you wanted to have sex with me to let me know before I fell asleep. Every time I look at you, you remind me of my mother's step father! And the things he did to me. And he kept doing it like I hadn't said anything. He tried to blame his impotency on me. I had been gone a year and a half so how could it have been my fault?

Anthony had gotten suspended from school again. I went to Alabama this time, and it was clear to me what I had to do, it was just a matter of when. It came on a day when he was getting on my motherfucking nerves. We were on our way home from River Oaks Mall. I started crying and he asked me what the problem was. I told him I couldn't do this anymore. I couldn't pretend that everything was alright. I didn't care how much money he had. I needed to get away, and I missed my other children. I had brought them in this world. They were my responsibility so I had to do what I had to do. The more I tried to explain, the less he understood. I told him, that my decision had nothing to do with him he was a good man, and I tried, Lord knows I did! But I couldn't keep letting him touch me or pretending that I enjoyed the things he did to me. I felt like I was suffocating and if I didn't get out soon I would surely die. I talked to Vee the night before and told her what I had planned on doing. She told me whatever my decision was, she was riding with me. March 29, 2004. Twenty three days after my third anniversary. I didn't think. I just started putting things into action. I called my supervisor at the hotel and let them know that I wouldn't be coming back. I then went to my little twin's school and checked them out and got their transfer. I went back home and started packing our clothes, as much as I thought would fit in my car. Chicago had bought me this piece of shit Grand Am. This was another way of him letting me know he was in control. He had a 1999 explorer. I had been asking him for the longest to buy me a car so I could do what I had to do, and not be dependent on him. The kind of money he had he could have bought five or six brand new cars. He further insulted me by running to his safe-deposit boxes. When I asked him what he was doing he said that he was putting protection on his money. I told him "if I had wanted to take something from you, it would have been gone by now! That's why your going to continue to be lonely cause money can't buy happiness or peace."

He went on and on as I was putting things in my car, saying "we need to talk." I said that is the problem, I've been talking all this time. You just haven't been listening. As I pulled away from the condominium complex. I felt as if a boulder had been lifted from my heart. My babies were content as long as they were with me they were alright. Cadesia reminded me of a little old lady. She had her hair tied down with a bandana, and her game boy. Lee was in the back seat, my comedienne, with a big smile on his face. Not once did they ask me where we were going. The only money I left with was two thousand dollars on my Citibank card, five hundred and eighty dollars in my purse. My State Farm agent had assured me that the check from my life insurance policy which I had cashed in would be mailed to me in two to three weeks.

My journey began. My car started giving me a little trouble as soon as I crossed over the Indiana state line. I stopped at a mechanic; he told me there was nothing wrong. By the time I reached Lebanon, Indiana my car had stopped on a dark ass highway. My cell phone only had like two bars left on it. I couldn't charge it because the lighter did not work in the car. I called Chicago and as soon as he opened his mouth I knew it had been a mistake. He said he knew the car wouldn't make it, that's what I get. That was the last thing I heard before I hung up. He was wasting my signals. Finally I called 911. I asked for assistance, after a couple of minutes a State Trooper came with a tow truck. They took us to the next exit where I got a room at a hotel. To the twins this was an adventure, they never complained.

Chicago called me back to see where we were. I asked him just out of curiosity would he go and put some money on my Citibank card. He told me "no, because I had made my decision." He just had given me another reason to dislike him. I asked him "How could you open your mouth to tell me you love me, and at the same time wish me to fail knowing that I had the children on the road with me?" He wasn't in control anymore and that irked the shit out of him. At the same time I wondered how the fuck I had stayed with this nigga for so long. The next morning, I called Enterprise. They sent an agent around with a car. I transferred all our things into the other car, I took my tags off, and we left Indiana around twelve. I could now plug my cell phone in to be charged. All down the highway I had friends talking to me Vee, my sister even Chicago called I guess out of morbid curiosity.

I knew he had called his mentor in New York, and another older friend in Birmingham. They were older friends of Chicago's and their opinion meant so much to him. He always needed their approval or okay to justify if he was right or wrong. And that was one of the reasons his ass was sitting in that house alone now. We made it to Birmingham around 8:00 pm. I drove to Bessemer to Vee's house; my other children were staying there. I was so tired all I wanted to do was to bathe and get into bed. The next couple of days entailed me driving Vee to work every morning, picking up Patricia, Anthony, and Nuke from Norwood. Then trying to get Lee and Cadesia into school. With that out the way I began to look for me a job. While looking for employment I had constant calls from Chicago trying to tear down the wall I had built. Then on top of all that, I wasn't giving Vee the kind of time she felt that she needed. My head wasn't in the right place and I explained that to her. I told her to let me get myself together, get me a place to stay, get me a car, and a job then I could give that some attention.

Apparently that wasn't good enough so she started doing her own thing, which was cool with me. By this time I had bought a little used car and was working at a hotel Vestavia. My friend Cheryl was being really good to me on top of helping out when I needed her to with the kids. She wanted a relationship too, but I told her that "I think we'd be better off as friends." She agreed and the tension was gone. Vee had started kicking it with Chicago on the phone. I guess she felt that she would be able to sabotage anything that was going on with me and him. She made a really bad mistake, because Chicago only wanted to prove to me that she wasn't my friend. Once he got her to talk to him for long periods of time she knew that he could play her. Dropping hints to him like I was jealous because she was seeing someone, and that I went and bought the same kind of car she bought. The sad part about it, everything that she told him, he'd turn right back around and tell me. I started wondering to myself if I could ever find someone to kick it with, someone who I could bare my soul with. Without being crossed.

At any rate I tried even harder now to find me a house, because in a minute I was going to blow. Not because she would tell him things, but because I thought we were friends. I gave her an example when I confronted her. I said, "If your woman called me and asked me where you were or what's going on?" Because you were my friend I would have to say, I think you need to ask her, and that I didn't want to get involved." She hurt me because I thought if it was one person I could trust it would have been her.

I had been working at the hotel now for a minute, and I knew I had to move out of Vee's house sooner not later. Chicago called me and asked me if I wanted to make some money. Because I needed money right away I told him, yes. Big mistake. He needed me to take care of some things over the weekend, and then I would be back in Birmingham by Sunday. For him that was a way of keeping tabs on me, but for me it was a way for me to come up real fast. Chicago thought that if we were around each other that we probably could re-kindle what we had. He didn't have a clue and that infuriated me even more. Also, because I knew I would have to have sex with him, it made me even angrier with myself. I had asked him one time why would it be so had for him and me to be friends? He was friends with all his other ex's so why couldn't it be so with us?

Once again I was going against what I believed. I started flying up every weekend taking care of some things for him, each time, and no sooner had I stepped of the plane, I was ready to go home again. I was always telling people to keep it real, but I realized that I was being a hypocrite because I was not keeping it real with Chicago or myself. Sometimes at night I would

TONI SHEALEY

lay in bed wondering, when was it ever going to be enough? Was I put on this earth to run into one brick wall after another? With Cheryl's help I finally found me a three bedroom house in Ensley. I called the landlord and she told me that she would meet with me on a Monday. Chicago told me that if I found a place he would help me with it. His main concern was what neighborhood it was in. Like he had grown up on the east side of Manhattan. I told him that I liked it and it would move me and my children out of Vee's house. He asked me how much the rent was. I told him. He told me that he would send me the money for a deposit and two months rent. The landlord was nice.

After our introductions I got straight to the point, "my credit isn't good at all, but I'm a good tenant and I pay on time." I have two months rent and a deposit. I really need a place to stay." She said she liked the way I came to her, we signed a lease. The house was mine for a whole year. I went to work immediately on my house. Cheryl helped me paint all the rooms; Chicago gave me money for a washer and dryer, a refridegerator and a stove. Cheryl knew a guy that fixed things and he would do it for a good price.

It was about a month in a half that I finished all the renovations and moved in. I made sure my children had beds first and I slept on the floor in my room on my new carpet. I was so proud of the house. My children had started new schools and made new friends. Before I got my living room furniture we would play cards on Friday and Saturday nights. I finally go my bedroom, and living room furniture delivered. My bedroom was my favorite place because I had a recliner over in a corner where I could sit back relax and read a book.

Chicago flew down after one of his trips just to see what kind of place I had. Then I became nervous because I knew he would have something negative to say and hurt my feelings. I picked him up from the airport then I went home. His mentor was down in Birmingham and Chicago was supposed to meet with him while he was here. The first thing he said when he goes in my room was "why is the bed so little?" (It was a full size bed) I said, "maybe because don't nobody sleep in it but me." Anything he said always made me second guess myself, and put me on the defensive. I wasn't going to back down this time. I let him know that my children didn't have a problem with our house, and I felt like I had done well for me and mine. I wasn't in anybody else's house it was mine!

Basically, I really did not give a damn about what he said, we like it and that was all that mattered. I was slowly detaching my way from him. Finally his visit came to an end. We agreed that I would see him after the fourth of July to take care of some things. I got Cheryl to babysit for me; sometimes I would be gone for five or six days. Also my cousin had got out of prison and he was staying with me. He was a responsible twenty two years old. He started going to college, and he was working at a barbershop trying to get himself together my children loved him.

In a way Duc Duc was still a kid himself. He helped me with them and anything I needed him to do he would. My sister Trice and my cousin had started hanging out at my house. They would try to get me to go to clubs but I just wasn't feeling that. Most of the time everyone just hung out at my house drinking beer, and having fun. On any given weekend you could find at least ten children in my house. I loved children, and I loved to see them happy.

My mama was in prison in New Jersey, I made sure she had all the things she needed to be comfortable. She had been having trouble with her health. Ironically, after all the shit we had been through, I was the one the responsibility fell on. No matter what she had did in my life she was still my mama.

I flew up there in August because she had, had a major surgery. Chicago was kind enough to meet me in New York. We rented a car and drove to New Jersey, and visited her on a Wednesday and Friday. When she seen Chicago and I it was like she had seen a ghost. Her eyes were closed because she was under so much medication, when she seen me standing in the door of her hospital room, tears was running down her face. I said, "You didn't think I was coming did you?" At that point I knew I had forgiven my mom for whatever part she played in my life and I had also forgiven myself. I was tired of holding grudges. I knew deep down in her heart she loved me and my sister, but she had her way and we had to accept that. Hell, I was almost forty years old. What was past was past and I couldn't do it over. I had learned hard lessons along the way, and I still had a ways to go.

While visiting my mom in New Jersey. I also had a chance to see and hangout with some of my old friends. This was 2004; we had come a long way from the Riverton. It had been twenty years. I was like, damn time flys. I met up with Coco, and Vern they were two of the people I had worked with and got high with. Twenty years later they were looking good and doing well. Some people, time and circumstances hadn't been too kind to them. Adele, Country and a whole lot of others had just said fuck it. I ran into Greasy she was one of the veteran females I had always looked up to. She was looking had good, but she had a tumor in her head. My son's father Sonny Boy had aged gracefully, but he was battling prostate cancer.

He came in the beauty shop and asked me, "Where is my boy?" I wasn't even mad at him any more. I didn't have the energy. It was not for me to deal with him. God already was. I told him what had happened concerning Willie, but I assured him that he was alright. I called my friend Goldie, she had wanted me to come to Brooklyn to see her, but I had already promised Vern and Coco that we were going out to dinner, and besides that we were leaving the next day. A lot of my mama's old friends had passed. Some had gotten their shit together:

I stopped and took a look at Harlem. I could not believe that I had been a part of this years ago. It had changed and it was beautiful. I looked over across the street to 7th avenue, and instead of abandoned buildings. I saw a store, a health food restaurant and a spa. I went over to the spa and got me a facial, and a full body massage. I bought all the products the young lady had used on my face. Coco, Vern and I had a passion for reading. Vern told me about this book named "Homo Thug" While she and Coco were getting their hair done for a wedding the next day I walked up to 125th and it engulfed me. The food, the smells, the people, oh my God I loved it. Every step I took, there were book stands with every black author you could imagine. I don't think I found "Homo Thug" but I walked away with about 20 books. Angel, me and my Boyfriend, True to the Game, B-more Careful, Imagine this and a whole lot more. I was like a baby in a toy store. I had read every book imaginable in and out of prison, but I had never seen the quantity of Black Author books that I seen that day. Finally I went back down on the Ave. Coco and Vern were ready. They wanted to go pick up Supreme. He and I used to kick it. He was a creep kid out of Queens and he hung at the hotel too. We also had a lot of fun together. We headed to Queens, laughing and reminiscing along the way. I called Chicago to let him know that I was going out to eat. When we got to Queens I med Cocos husband and seen her nice house. We went to pick up Supreme. We went inside to speak to his mom and also his brother Born. Born was a baller back in the days but fate had dealt him a bad hand he was paralyzed from the waste down. We ended up going to Applebee's. We sat there and reminisced until the place closed. Then we all cried for the still sick and suffering and for us to be still standing. Chicago and I left the next day. I had visited my mom again that Friday and the doctors assured me that she was going to be fine.

Chicago flew back to Chicago and me to Birmingham. For the next couple of months I would fly back and forth to Chicago to Birmingham, but it was wearing me down, and I was tired of playing with Chicago. I got a call one day from him asking me if I had anybody in mind that was respectable and articulate. I told him yeah. So I called my friend India and asked her did she want to take a trip? She had been bugging me forever, so now was her chance. India and I few to Chicago on a Saturday night. Chicago picked us up from Midway airport. I was really tired, but once we got back to the condo, I had to put some things together. Once, I finished it was about 12:01 am I took me a shower, gave India towels and stuff. Then I went in the room to go to sleep. I kept hearing a notice in my sleep. When I finally realized what it was. I was like "no this motherfucker ain't what I heard was the television and one sound coming from it was a porn tape with people having sex. Then I heard Chicago tell India, "Get that" I was so ashamed and embarrassed that I never even opened my eyes when he pulled my legs apart. I kept thinking to myself, "Do you actually thing that he would change?" After they finished I just rolled over and went to sleep with tears rolling down my face. The next day we flew over to Ohio, one of Chicago friends picked us up. She dropped us off at the hotel and said that she'd send a driver the next morning? I thought that this maniac had got all the sex out of his system. When we lay down to go to sleep India was in the recliner. I'm usually a hard sleeper, but this time I woke right up. The didn't know that I was up, and I wasn't going to let them know either. I turned over to get in a comfortable position, and then I started snoring for added effect so he could think I was still sleep. He had pushed India head down to where she could lick and suck on this nipples like a bitch! While she was doing that, he was getting his self off, jacking his dick. By the time I thought he was getting ready to have an orgasm I hit that nigga dead in the back of his head. I startled him so bad; I thought he was going to have a heart attack. It really would have been funny if it wasn't so sad. I really could not take it anymore! I said, "If you wanted me to bring someone to freak with that's what you should have said. I brought this girl up here for business not for you to have sex with! Then you assumed I felt it would be alright. I let that shit slide the night before last but it's beginning to be too much." He was standing there embarrassed because he had got caught. He said "You don't have to talk to me like that." I said "you shouldn't have done what you did then." I looked over at India and she looked like a scared dear. I told her I was not angry with her. My husband had led her to believe this was some initiation. Then I really got pissed off because now I would have to deal with India in case she went back to Birmingham saying "I slept with Toni's husband!" He was truly pathetic. I told him before I came home from prison that he had to be tested for HIV or any other communicable diseases and that he needed to send me the results. And he did.

But I started wondering once I got home if he had been with other females while I was away, because now it seemed like he was obsessed with sex. The next day after we finished working. I put India on a plane back to Birmingham. I really felt bad about how the situation had turned out. I had pumped this nigga up like he was strictly about business, but he made me out of a liar. When I got back to the hotel he gave me some gold earrings he had brought and an ankle bracelet. I guess that was his way of apologizing. I wasn't feeling it. From that point on being around him exhausted me because I was constantly fronting like very thing was alright and it wasn't. It had gotten to the point that I hated even to be around him. I remember that last night we were together. After the India incident I wouldn't have sex with him. After I showered I got in one bed and fell asleep. I woke up and I felt his hands on my breast. I wanted to throw up. I asked him not to touch me, then I went back to sleep. Before we departed at the airport he told me that the next weekend he would be going to Georgia, to get Heaven to go on the road. Like I really gave a fuck. That would be the last time that I went with him.

I was glad to be back in Birmingham, and settled back into my mama role. Patricia was in the Ensley band. October was the time the big events came to Birmingham. The Battle of The Bands which Patricia was in, the Classics Parades, a whole lot of different things. On the weekends, all of my friends would all end up at my house or one of the others, just to drink beer, play cards, just chill. Jay was one of Vee's friends. I had seen her over the years at different functions we both attended. Here lately I was seeing a lot more of her. She had played the music for Vee's birthday in April, and I seen her again at another friend of Vee.

The impression I got from her was that she was laid back, she never said too much of anything unless you addressed her, then she smiled, she lit up a whole room. One night we were all sitting on my front porch having a good time, taking pictures and talking about all kinds of things we had all been through. My cousin was over there too. At the time she was going through changes with her girl so more than ever she would be at my house. After we kicked it for a little while longer, everybody were collecting their shit, cleaning up, and getting ready to pull out. I told Jay, "You don't have to leave because they are." You would have thought I started World War I. Everybody started talking at one time. They were like, "No, Jay come on. Toni leave my friend alone." My cousin said, "Toni don't bother her." I was tripping like what the fuck is up? So I looked at Jay and said, "Go, they act like you're a child or something." She was like, "I'm grown. I do what I want to do." She was helping me put stuff in the house. I told her to "Go ahead, I got it!" I was pissed off actually more at myself than any thing. Because people perceived me as being callous and uncaring, also inconsiderate of other females feelings. Don't get me wrong. I was attracted to females but I didn't want the attachment that came with it. There were times when Vee and I still slept with each other but the next day we would be back to our old selves like nothing had happened. If Vee was in a relationship though we never disrespected that. I guess that's what pissed me off so bad with her girlfriends. Vee and I talked about a lot of things, but that was it. All her girlfriends were very intimidated by me.

I loved my children with all my heart and soul, so if one of them didn't care for you, your ass had to step. And that was cool because all I needed was them. I wasn't desperate for no companionship. Chicago had been calling me for a while, so I finally told him that I wouldn't be coming back. We were suppose to go to Vegas after Christmas but I was enjoying my independence and I told him I didn't want to be with him anymore of course he thought I was kidding, because I had told him that before, he was in for a rude awakening. I started going out to the clubs. I got tired of, my friends saying, "All I did was stay in the house"

The first time I went out. We went to a strip club downtown it was a popular strip club in Birmingham. I went with my sister and cousin. Amazingly I had a nice time. I was not a club person. I would be satisfied just sitting in my house reading, watching, and television. Or just enjoying my children. I joined a Women's Fit Club, I went to the beauty shop religiously every Saturday and the nail shop every two weeks. That was my idea of entertainment. I went out another time with Vee, Betty, my cousin, and my Trice. We ran into Jay down there that night. There was one stripper that caught my eye. She was a Caucasian; she made those black girls in there that night look like a fool. I sent Betty for change at least three times. After a while I started tipping her with ten's and twenties. I enjoyed myself tremendously that night.

Vee called me again the next weekend and asked me if I wanted to go to this gay club. Some of my other gay friends had been trying to get me to go forever so I said, "sure, why not?" Vee, drove to my house and we drove my truck down. I called my cousin to see if she was going, she said that she would meet me down there. It was my first time ever going in there. The music was jumping after I had me about two Budlights; I was definitely feeling the music. Vee was enjoying herself too. My cousin came in. Then I noticed my other cousin, in there and we were all having a good time. The Dee Jay put on "Everybody in the Club Gettin Tipsy" by Chingy. That was one of my favorite songs, and I was feeling it. The next thing I know, I feel someone dancing on my back. I was getting ready to straight snap until I turned around and realized it was Jay.

All of a sudden something clicked, she was looking good like a motherfucker, and the attraction I felt for her left me breathless. Anytime I was around Jay in the past she was always low key, and as I watched her dance she even did that cool. I took her jacket so she could get comfortable dancing. I was enjoying watching her. Three of Jay's friends had come to the club with her: I spoke to them all. I had actually met one of them in 2001, when she and my cousin were together.

A slow song comes on Jay and I looked up at each other at the same time. I asked her friend to hold Jay's jacket for me, and we slow danced. To me there was no one there but her and me. I was on fire; she had no idea of the turbulence going on in my head. The song ended we went back to our seats. She stood behind me, and I couldn't think of a better place I would have liked to be than right there. Vee had been telling me all night "You and Jay ought to hook-up." I didn't dispute because I was definitely feeling her. I noticed that Vee had, had her share of drinks so it was time for us to dip. I let my cousins know that we were leaving, and to see if they were okay. Jay and her crew were leaving too! It was pretty cold outside but Jay walked me over to my truck. Her friends were yelling for her to come on because they had rode with her to the club and it was cold as hell out side.

I got in the truck, Jay gave me her number, and I gave her mine. We talked for a few minutes then I leaned over and kissed her. I surprised myself more than I did her. What was really scary was that the last time I had feelings of this nature. I was in love. I had to give this situation further thought. We parted with the promise of calling each other. As I was driving home Vee said, "I'll kill you bitch!" She was drunk so I didn't pay her any mind.

The following week I was preparing to give Patricia, my niece Diona, Chicago's daughter and Chicago's little cousin a sleep over at the Embassy Suites. His cousin was flying in from Chicago, and his daughter was coming from Alexander City. I had also reserved a room next door to theirs for the adults. Jay had been calling all week and I kept coming up with one excuse after the other. Bottom line was I had fallen for ole girl just that fast, and I was scared, because when I love, I love hard. I just didn't have the energy to be emotionally involved or so I thought. I'm not the type of person to think that you have to be with a person five years to say you are in love. I believed in love at first sight.

I can say one thing about her, she never gave up. I got a call from her on Friday, and into our conversation I told her that I had to pick Chicago's cousin up from the airport. She told me that she would pick her up for me since it was on her side of town. It was also a big help for me because I still had a lot of running around to do. At six o'clock every body started showing up at the hotel. I had ordered the girls pizza and wings in every flavor. They had a boom box in their room, and they were going to go swimming later.

The adults played cards, drank beer, and periodically got up and checked on the girls. More so now cause our bad ass boys had crashed the girl's party. We had to tell them to keep it down a couple of times. Around 12:30 am everything was winding down. We cleaned up, made sure we had a head count on the girls, got Duc Duc to take the boys to my house and then everyone else left. Everyone except for Jay. It was a relief to me that everyone was gone because I had made up in my mind that it was going down. I couldn't fight my attraction to Jay any longer. I decided to let fate do what it had to do. I took a shower. I was kind of nervous but I was going for all or nothing. I walked back in the room Jay was sitting on the couch. I put my feet in her lap. Till this day I couldn't tell you what we talked about because I wanted her that bad. We kissed and then after awhile. I said let's pull out the couch. November 19, 2004 we consummated our relationship.

The next morning I had no regrets or trepidations. Which was odd for me. Usually, after I sleep with someone I feel detached. But this morning, I felt good. We got the girls up to freshen up, and to go downstairs to eat breakfast. Chicago called me to check and see how their sleep over went. I told him. Then he told me to go ahead keep both rooms he would pay for it since the girls enjoyed themselves so much.

Needless to say Jay and I became inseparable after that night. I would drive over to her house after nine when my small kids had been put to bed. Then I would drive back home around six a.m. before they got up to get ready for school. Duc Duc would stay at the house with them. Some nights she'd stay at my house, she and her brother Mayo.

Jay and I had become comfortable with each other and we shared a lot of things. I never questioned the relationship because it felt right. The paid attention to my needs, and she made it about me. It's really hard to explain it. I just knew that were I was suppose to be. I had to go out of town for a week the first part of December. This time instead of Cheryl watching my

TONI SHEALEY

kids Jay stayed over. She took me to the airport and as I was going through the line. I turned around; she was standing there waiting for me to go through. I went through the metal detector, I turned around and waved again, she waved back, and then turned around to leave. I turned around once more and she was gone. I felt like the breath had been knocked out of me. I was so weak! As I sat there waiting for my plane. I text paged her and told her I loved her. I wasn't going to send it at first because I didn't want to scare her off, but I wanted her to know how I felt. Through out my life I had dealt with females on and off mostly in prison. Never had I openly, in public, for fear of what people may say. Jay created feelings in me that were refreshing, that had me anticipating seeing her again, to be in her arms. I didn't give a fuck what people said. For once in my life I was truly happy. My children were also. I had an open and honest relationship with them especially the big twins. When I came back from my trip we discussed our feelings, she did send me a return text message saying that she loved me.

It was almost Christmas time and my tree was packed. Mostly with things for my smaller kids. The big twins told me everything they wanted so most of my shopping was for Jay, Mayo and friends. I would get so excited after I bought Jay something and tell her to open it right then. Chicago had come to Birmingham to pick up Hassan and to visit his friend. We really didn't talk much. I just got in the truck and drove off. Jay and I had talked about moving in with each other. I was getting ready to move out the house I was in after New Year's. Because of our love for each other we decided that I'd move over with her, me and the kids.

She bought my kids everything they asked her for for Christmas and they got along pretty well. When I told them we were moving after New Years. Patricia got an attitude. She told me she didn't want to leave Ensley. I told her when she got her a job and a house then she could run shit, but until then I was in control. I had met the majority of Jay's friends and they were so down to earth they accepted me with open arms. I knew that they loved Jay tremendously and it showed. I got sick that night and before we finished opening up all the gifts I was falling out of the chair. I asked Jay to apologize for me, but they understood. We ended up going back to my house because we wanted to be there when the kids opened their gifts. That was another reason I was in love with Jay. She romanced me, and she was very considerate of my needs. She wasn't a big talker which infuriated me at times, but she let me know she loved me with her actions.

The following weekend was New Year's Eve and Jay's birthday. We had reserved like eight or nine rooms. She had friends coming from Atlanta;

I had invited people it was jumping. We had food, drinks, and the whole nine. After the count down everyone got dressed to go to the club. The club was packed. We had so much fun. The next morning all of us got up trying to find somewhere to go for breakfast. We had driven to several IHOPs, and they all were packed. So we ended up going to Shoney's on the southside. Our wait was about two or three minutes. Soon the waitress came and led us to an area like a conference room, because it was a lot of us. After the waitress took our order. I just happened to look up and noticed that the people at the next table were staring. I mean they stopped eating and looked at us like we had horns on our head. I got angry because if you're going to stare at least put some shade on it. I said out loud. "I wonder why those people are staring at us. Surely they've seen lesbians before, or have someone in their family that is gay, a crackhead, or even in jail!" Once they realized I was talking to them they picked up their utensils and began to eat again. Finally our food came. Everybody was talking about how good of a time they had and about our upcoming trip to Cancun. My cell phone rang and it was Chicago letting me know that he had took Hassan home. I told Ebony I'll meet her back at her house. I wanted to spend a little more time with her because I was leaving the next day.

When I got to my house Chicago was already there. He told me that he was leaving today because he didn't want to be at the airport at the same time with me. It irked the shit out of him to know that I knew a lot more than he did. He gave me a gift. I opened it up in front of him. He had bought me two nice Nike jogging suits. I told him thank you. He asked me was I sure that this is what I wanted to do. Meaning the separation. I told him "yes." A part of me knew that Chicago had been sleeping with someone else because he was a sex addict, plus he always needed to have a female around him to validate his self and for appearances. He let me know in so many words that, "I would be nothing without him." It was too late he couldn't hurt me anymore, and whoever he was with God bless them. Chicago needed to be needed that's the only way he could feel good about himself. I got up from my sofa which was an indication that I was through talking to him. He said, "So you're not going to interfere in my life? I said "NO!" He said well, because I got a woman. I said, "I do too!" That really fucked him up. So he had to come back with something more powerful. He said, "Vee told my friend that you were smoking crack." Before I knew it I had hit him with my cell phone. He said that because he knew it would bother me. Of course he said, Vee said it! Then I wouldn't have put it pass her either. She stopped speaking to me and Jay and claimed it was because she dated us both. That was a bunch of bullshit! She knew that once I started kicking it with someone on the regular. It was over. No more late night creeps or nothing. Chicago was still standing in my door. I had told him to leave and he still stood there. I went in the kitchen to get a knife. Patricia ran in there and grabbed Chicago. She said, "Chicago, please go on!" From that point on the only time he and I ever talked was concerning Hassan.

Vee had told me that if Jay and I were ever at an event she would leave. I mean she was taking this shit to the extreme. But once she realized that we were going to be together. She went on to another topic. Finally the day came for us to move. We rented a U-haul loaded everything on there and on my van and made one trip. The next day I had to go register the children for school When Patricia realized that a bunch of her friends went to Huffman she calmed her little self down. Anthony didn't mind one way or the other as long as he was with me. The little one's were just happy, especially Hassan because he stayed with his daddy's people for ten years and this would be the first time that he lived with me permanently since he was eight months old.

Mayo had to get use to sharing his space and his sister, but it all worked out in the end. February 1, 2005 came around and everyday I would find something on my pillow, or hints to find a gift somewhere in the house. I got a gift everyday from her up until February 14th. For Valentine's Day she took me to a very exclusive hotel downtown called the Tutwiler. When the bell boy opened the door to the room, there were rose petals, starting at the door ending at the bed. On the bed were big juicey strawberries dipped in chocolate, there was a balcony in the bedroom and the living room. She had also bought me this really cute pink and white outfit from finish line and some pink and white shocks. Prior to meeting Jay I never had experienced a lot of things sexually. Well, she broadened my horizons and I caught on like wildfire. One of our friends Sunshine would say I was "so gay" because when I talked about Jay and I, I always had this big stupid grin on my face. I wanted to let the whole world know.

We went to the club that night but we didn't enjoy it because some one got into a fight, and the police sprayed pepper spray into the whole club, so we left. Besides that I enjoyed my evening. Before we left the next morning we ate a nice breakfast. I appreciated this girl so fucking much because in all my thirty eight years I never had anyone to treat me as special as she had. And a lot of times I would shut her out because that shit from the past would grip me and I didn't want to be intimate with her.

But being the person that she is, she remembered things I told her and she never pressured me about it. I think we both figured out what if I initiated the intimacy then I wouldn't feel threatened. At any rate she understood. She never pressured me, or talked down to me, or used my past to hurt me. To me Jay was my logical side. Where I was intense, she was laid back. I always had to have shit done right then, it took her a little more time, but she got it done. After Valentine's Day I decided to get a job. I was also going to enroll in school to study business. I went to Birmingham Health Care, where my sister was the executive assistant to the CEO. I filled out an application and fortunately the lady that did the hiring interviewed me. She told me she would call me as soon as she spoke with the CEO.

She needed to verify if it was okay to hire me because my sister worked there. I left there and went to Pelham to register for my classes at Faulker University. I stopped at a shell service station to get a soda and some gas. My cell phone rang and I answered. It was my sister. She asked me where was I. Then she asked me when could I start? I said, "When do they want me to start?" she said "Tomorrow at the dental clinic. I would be filling in for another employee until she finished taking her bar exams. From there I would go to Metro. I was so happy. I couldn't contain myself. I couldn't wait to tell Jay.

She had resigned from her job to find something better. But she was happy for me too. One thing about Jay, she was very considerate of me. She encouraged me and she supported me in my efforts. She constantly told me that I could do anything I wanted to do once I put my mind to it. My hours were from 7:30 to 4:30.

One day when I came home from work all six of the children were standing at the bottom of the basement steps, watching me as I got out of the car. I asked them "what was wrong?" "They said, "That they were so proud of me, working." I cried so hard that day because I never knew how much my children worried about me going on the road and not coming back until that day.

My sister would come and we would do lunch at the clinic or go to my Aunties house. Jay had found her a job, and it was really long hours. Sometimes she wouldn't get home until 9:30 or 10:00 at night, and she would be really tired once she got there! My hours were 8 to 5 p.m now. A lot of times I wouldn't get home until about 6 p.m. It depended on if I had to stop at the store or something. When I got home. I didn't take a shower right away because I had to talk to each child in detail of what their day was like. Then I would cook if I felt like it, if not Patricia would.

Jay would come home on Friday and see a bunch of kids; she never asked any questions because she knew I had sent for them. My heart was my cousin's stepson Fat Daddy, and my co worker's son Geordan. Those two little boys could just look at me and my heart would melt.

Chicago had started phone stalking again. He had a new girl friend now and he wanted me to know it. He went so far as to have her to call me and ask me when I was coming to Chicago. I said never but I realized she just didn't decide to pick up the phone and say, "I think I'll call Toni." I waited for a while before I called back and I asked him, "Why did you have that girl call my house?" He was like, "she called your house?" As if he didn't know. I heard her in the background saying, "Chicago you told me to call her!" I said" let me speak to her." He gave her the phone. I said," I know Chicago told you to call me and I ain't mad at you. He's messy just like a bitch. All he wants you to do is pull on that little penis and lick on his nipples with his nasty ass. Did he tell you I left him, he didn't leave me. He wants you to feel like you are in competition with me! You're not! I have a woman and I'm happy so you all have a nice day."

I hung up the phone. I looked around Jay and the bigger kids were killing themselves laughing. I had found a job that I loved at Metro. I loved caring and dealing with people. A lot of people I knew were in prison with, or who had just grew up together. The newer clients would look at me and say, you just don't understand. I would tell them I understand way more than you think. I tell them a little of my story, to make them feel comfortable and for them to know I had walked in those shoes. So it was okay at least they were trying to get help. The people I was in prison with would see I and they would be embarrassed, but I told them I was still the same Toni that they knew, and they had no reason to be embarrassed. I remember one day a girl named Winkie came in because someone told her I worked there. She was trying to describe me to Tawanda the receptionist, but Winkie was getting frustrated so finally she said we were in prison together. I was laughing when Tawanda told me. I said it was a good thing you all knew I had been in prison.

That following Sunday was the Sunday that Mayo, Lee and Cadesia got baptized, of course I cried. The next Sunday was Easter Sunday. We went to church and then we went home had dinner, around five we went to the park because we had a game to play. I had made a lot of friends at work with my co workers they were all really down to earth people. Kim and Dee were my dawgz, my buddies Kim worked upstairs in Medical, and Dee was in Medical records. Dee was famous for saying, "Let it Burn" and I picked it up. Jay's friend son would kill himself laughing when I said that.

I had no complaints, all my life I dreamed of being able to do something that I would enjoy, and I had found it. I was getting ready to register for the fall semester at Jeff State to take social work, or administrative assistant. I was really good with learning different software, or just learning period. Jay always encouraged me to follow my dreams. Sometime we would lie in bed at night and I would tell her about my past. She would say, "Baby, you need to write a book!" I would laugh it off but she was dead ass serious.

Our life together had become comfortable. I had no qualms about the choice I had made I asked my daughter, Patricia, if she minded the fact that Jay and I was together? She said, "No, both of you are here!" So that's what maters to them. I had ordered them a book from Amazon.com called "Children of Gay Parents" All three of the big kids read it. That was one of my main concerns, wondering how my children would cope with me living openly with a woman. They loved Jay to death. All of Jay friends had adopted us too. Her family was crazy about them, and didn't treat them any different from the others. Dee was all my kids favorite because he played with them but when it came time for business he'd lay one of them out in a heartbeat.

Jay didn't know what becoming a family with her did for my kids and me. Her family made us their family, and her friends made us theirs. I had never seen my kids smile so much in their life. When I say family and friends these people were dedicated. In a pinch, I could pick up the phone and call anyone of them and they'd be there. I had never been so content in my life. I wonder sometimes if the molestation or rapes damaged me and my perceptions of men. Even though I had been with numerous men. I was never able to feel the oneness or wholeness that I have with Jay. I told her once that my life depended on the air she breathed.

A lot of times I wasn't able to show it because I felt if I did she would go away. I still had some of those insecurities from the past.

We went to church Sunday and I was really enjoying the sermon. I remember the pastor saying, "Have you felt alone all your life?" Were you tired of people saying you were never going to be nothing?" When I looked up I was at the alter tears were streaming down my face as the spirit worked with me. I felt as if a boulder had been lifted from my shoulders, like I had been carrying it around all these years. My children were standing Jay was standing and rejoicing. Anybody that knew me, and knew the life I had led, the pain I endured, they knew that I was freeing myself, and I didn't owe

TONI SHEALEY

nobody nothing but me, and the family we built. When I left out of that church that day my step was a little lighter, and my smile a little brighter. I loved my life, my family and my job and that was ll that mattered and that I worked with Jay as one to keep and maintain our family.

Mother's Day came around and Jay and the kids once again set it out for me. Anything that I said I wanted leading up to Mother's Day I got it. Jay even bought the tag for my car it says "Mz. Toni" I was so proud of my tag. I showed everybody at work! A mess! I bought Jay a cell phone for Mother's Day. She had planned to take me out to whatever restaurant I wanted to go to. But we decided to go to Ryan's so the kids could go too. Her friend and her son went with us too.

We had one more week before we left for Cancun I was so excited because I had never been out of the country. I had been packing our stuff all week. Monday the 16th of May, after I got off work I went and got my nails done. Tuesday, I went to the shop and let Tassity lock my hair nobody, did short hair like Ms. Thing. Wednesday I left work with promises of bringing back gifts. I picked up my auntie, stopped at the grocery store, and then headed home. Auntie was keeping the kids while we were gone. I gave Auntie and Patricia last minute instructions.

Jay got home changed clothes, we said our good byes. I did not know that this would be the last time that would I see them for a while. If I had of followed my instincts I never would have went. Earlier in April I got a call telling me that Chicago had been arrested by the Feds. Chicago's mentor told me that he didn't think that it was a good idea for me to go out of the country. He said he believed at the time of Chicago's arrest, that they had a warrant for me too. I was trying to figure out "why the fuck would I have a warrant?" I knew that in November of 2004 one of Chicago's friends had gotten arrested. He didn't tell me that his foundation was crumbling around him. About two weeks after he was arrested, he called me and said that the feds had taken some things out of his condo when they arrested him. Also, that the feds had taken some mail with my name on it. I asked him was this something I needed to be worried about? He told me no. His mentor called me again and said, he didn't think that I should go to Cancun because that's how one of his friends got apprehended. I told him that I wasn't worried about that cause if the feds wanted me they would have come to my house or job. We drove to Atlanta the night of the 18th. The next morning we took a shuttle to the airport where we waited on the others from Atlanta. We boarded our flight and arrived in Cancun about two hours later. Most of us slept going over because we were still tired from lack of sleep. Jay and I packed our DVD player, and I packed books. I kept falling asleep on the plane so I gave up. Once we got through customs and got our luggage. We were driven to our Hotel the Moon Palace. Our rooms weren't ready yet so we went in the dining room and ate.

There was so much food and the service was great. Then our tour gave us an orientation on the tours so we could choose the Carribean Cruise, the jungle ATV, and the shopping tour. After orientation we all went to our rooms to take a nap. I was hyped. I didn't want to miss nothing! I didn't even take a nap. Everybody met out front at 6:00. The van took us to fat Tuesday to bake a cruise over to the island. While we were waiting to board, we ordered drinks. I had a drink called a tropical itch, there was music playing and everything, music was even playing on the ship. We were getting tore the fuck up. On the island there was a buffet with all kind of food, we ate. Then the bartenders brought tequila shots over to our table. Out of the whole crew. I was the one that couldn't drink nothing but beer and mixed drinks, but I was like what the fuck give me a shot too. I was throwing them back like a pro.

. On our way back over to the main land. I danced so hard my breast jumped out of my halter. We were so drunk; half of us fell asleep on the way back to the hotel. I felt like I was on a honeymoon the air just had a different feel. Jay and I took time to explore each other more, and took advantage of not having to whisper. It was great, she and I in that room and it was pure bliss. We would enjoy the next three nights there also. The next morning we went on the jungle tour. When we got back to the hotel. Later on that evening we had a ceremony for Sunshine and her partner. The sun was setting, we all held candles for our friendship to them, and Jay officiated. It was beautiful, and it was something that I had never felt or witnessed before.

Our flight home seemed like it was quicker than the one we took over. Soon as we landed I turned my cell phone on and called home. Patricia answered the phone she said, "mama where you at?" I said, "We're getting off the plane now." She said, "How long is it going to take for y'all to get home? I said, "About two hours." The flight attendants were letting us know to take our identification and our birth certificate to show to the customs officer as we went through. As I got to the front of the line the officer said, "Ma'am could you step to the side?" He said, "There's a warrant for you in Ohio." I almost passed out. Jay was asking me what was going on. I told her they said I had a warrant in Ohio. All our other friends had already gone through except two. Jay asked the officer if they could

TONI SHEALEY

give me money. He said "yes" Jay handed me four hundred dollars that her friend gave her to make sure I had money. But none of this was making sense to me.

As we were walking. I used my cell phone to call back home. I told my daughter that they were taking me to jail. All hell broke loose. She started crying, my auntie got on the phone, then my cousin got on the phone. Shit was slowly unraveling around me. I felt as if this was happening to someone else. It couldn't possibly be happening to me! Once we got to the door of the officer station Jay hugged me and told me everything was going to be alright. I got inside; I called everyone to let them know what was going on.

Two agents came for me, confiscated all my personal belongings, and escorted me out of the airport in handcuffs. Back in the day I wouldn't have gave a fuck about being arrested. Things had changed. I was so embarrassed. The agents took me to ACDC a hold facility for Feds in Downtown Atlanta. A female officer searched me. I felt so degraded, I had done this a hundred times in my life, but it didn't feel like this. I tried to call Jay but her phone wasn't getting a signal. I called home, and finally I was able to talk to her on the three way. I really couldn't tell them anything. All I knew is that I had to be extradited back to Ohio to answer for these charges. I found out the next day at the federal building that I was being charged with Bank Fraud and Theft identity.

I had been in and out of prisons all my life but noting prepared me for the feds. They play emotional games with you leaving people at a facility for long periods of time, until you're just ready to snap. From the federal building I was transported to Union City Jail. I stayed there two weeks. During this time I was calling home because Patricia said she wasn't staying there. I asked her, "Where do you plan on going?" No where, I told her she had better sit her little narrow ass down somewhere, because she didn't run anything. She also had hurt Jay's feeling because she knew Jay would never do anything to harm them, but care for them as I did. But I also understood Patricia behavior because each time I went away the people I was with would separate them and me too. I got scared too, and in my heart I knew that Jay would stick by me. I couldn't even compare our relationship to any I had and she never gave me reason to believe otherwise.

In the beginning my sister, my cousins, a whole bunch of people that I had been true to made whole bunch of promises like they would be there for me, help Jay with the kids, the whole nine. After a while the list got shorter and shorter. I was hurt, but I knew that these people weren't going to help. In a way I'm glad that they didn't. For me it was one less bell to answer. The people I had, just me, my woman, and our friends are the ones that came through for me.

. After two weeks in Union City. I was transferred again to another jail in Georgia. Paulding County. It was nasty, I cried everyday and I questioned God. Why was this happening? Didn't I do all the things I was supposed to do? I was really freaking out. I missed Jay and the kids more and more each day. It got to a point where I couldn't get on the phone without crying. Another two weeks passed, and I and a bunch of other females were taken to the airstrip to get on the plane. This shit was wild. We flew to upstate New York some inmates got off, some got on. Then we flew to Pittsburgh, where I and two other females were taken to Medina County Jail. I've had a lot of time to think and reflect on my life. Jay's strength and encouragement had kept me strong. I've decided that God has put me here for a reason; maybe it was to write this book, or to except responsibility for what ever part I played. Whatever it is all I can do is to keep praying, believing that God will do what he sees fit for me. I don't hear much from nobody but Jay and the kids, and our friends. I'm okay with that because God has narrowed it down for me. The ones that stood by me will know that they have a friend for life because being in jail with out nothing and nobody is a painful thing. I thank God for my people. My journey is almost over I've been in jail now for four months. I go for sentencing on December 7, 2005. I'm not afraid. God knows my heart, and I truly believe that He won't give me more than I can bear. I plan on being home for Christmas. One day I'll be able to look back and reflect on this time because this was a valuable learning experience. Jay finally got a job she enjoys, the kids are all doing fine just being kids. Life has its ups and downs because we're not perfect. We all make mistakes, but there not mistakes anymore when you constantly do them over and over again. Me, I'm taking it one day at a time because if I constantly think about my situation. I'll drive myself crazy. I've discovered a whole lot of things since I've been here, and one of them is don't take you life for granted. You can be here today and gone tomorrow. I tell Jay I love her every chance I get, and my children. There are people out there pulling for me. This incarceration puts closure on this part of my life because the Toni is no more. I think I turned out pretty good, but I've always been a fighter. My job is done. I'm taking my life back. I WILL SUCCEED!!

TONI SHEALEY